Sun Brewing Company Cookbook Second Edition

Sun Brewing Company Cookbook Second Edition

Avant-Garde Brewing and Cooking with Beer from the Texas Border

David Slocum

CONTENTS

1. Acknowledgments & Advance Praise. 1
2. How to Read this Book. 5
3. Sundown on a Chapter in My Life. 7
4. PART ONE: THE STORY OF SUN BREWING 11
5. Becoming El Guapo. 12
6. PART TWO: COOKING WITH EL GUAPO 27
7. Cooking with Beer. 28
8. PART THREE: EL GUAPO'S BREW KETTLE 42
9. BAG Beers. 43
10. PART FOUR: EL GUAPO'S KITCHEN 167

CONTENTS

11 | Borderland Avant-garde and Fusion Food. 168

12 | Borderland Barbecue Recipes. 221

13 | Salads. 250

14 | Dressings. 254

15 | Sides. 256

16 | Beer Breads 263

17 | Sauces. 270

18 | Desserts. 287

19 | Final Thoughts. 293

20 | Letter to Fallen Marines. 309

21 | Tools and Resources. 315

22 | Glossary. 316

23 | List of Titles & Table of Recipes. 318

Copyright © 2022 by David Slocum

All rights reserved. No part of this book may be reproduced in any manner whatsoever without written permission except in the case of brief quotations embodied in critical articles and reviews.

First Printing, 2022

1

Acknowledgments & Advance Praise.

Acknowledgments.

Many people helped in crafting this book whether it was my wife watching the kids to allow me some writing time or my great team Brad Fruhauff from The Pen and Pint and Julie White from FRW Studios, who helped me tremendously reshape my book. I also want to thank Kristi Switzer from Brewers Publications, who was the first to read my manuscript years ago. She was very candid with me, and I appreciated that. Kristi told me I had written three books in one, which was the very beginning of many restructuring efforts over the years. I also want to thank Kristi for having recommended Brad and Julie because they're both a world-class talent, which is evident in this book's development.

We are but mere brewers... Rock On!

Sun Brewing is my love affair that lasts a life time.

Advance Praise.

Everyone has a friend named Dave, or at least, they should. Dave is that guy that comes to the neighborhood party with great homebrew and awesome food to share. For David Slocum, those brews and that food is the result of a rich childhood in the American South, his tours of duty in the US Marines, and his love of the culture and people of El Paso, Texas, and Juarez, Mexico. From these elements were born the desire to create, the pride and satisfaction of success, and the joy of giving back to the community that made it all possible. This book is the conversation you and Dave have standing next to the barbecue at the neighborhood cookout, the inside scoop on the Where, What and How of the fantastic flavors that is Sun Brewing Company. I can't wait to try these recipes!
– John Palmer, author of How To Brew

There can be no arguing: beer pairs far better and more extensively with food than does wine. There can be no better example than that given here, with passion and belief.
– Charlie Bamforth – The Pope of Foam
Distinguished Professor Emeritus
University of California Davis

This is definitely a must-have for anyone who likes cooking with beer. The book is very well written, and includes all sorts of wonderful information about craft beer and cooking, for newbies and veterans alike. David has inspired me as a business owner to put my recipes in writing. He has reminded nothing is impossible with his dedication to his award winning beers and recipes. As one of his culinary instructors at EPCC he has made me very proud of his achievements.

– Chef Angel Beasley owner of Sun City's Hawaiian Shave Ice and Chef Instructor at El Paso Community College in the Culinary Arts Department.

It's a rare thing to watch creativity at work. It's seldom neat and often makes you wonder what exactly is going on. The Sun Brewing Company Cookbook is a fine example of what I'm talking about. Is it a brewing guide? Is it a biography? Is it a cookbook? Yes. It is all three at once, which makes for an adventure. I've often thought of David Slocum, the author, as one of the most committed brewpub owners in the state of Texas. He's lived in his brewery at times, worked to learn increasingly complex brewing techniques all while cooking for his guests at Sun Brewing. He is always working to learn more. This book is evidence of how committed he is to his craft and to sharing what he's learned, which is a hallmark of the craft beer industry.

It's a bit audacious, in defining some hyper-local new styles based within (and on) the community where Sun Brewing is located. Tamarindo, Chamoy, Huitlacoche, Green Mole... These are not ordinary beer ingredients. Toss in some wild fermentation, some food recipes to pair with these audacious brews and you've got a microcosm of the furthest west you can get in Texas and the influences guiding beer there, not to mention the guiding philosophy of the man creating them, David Slocum.

The Sun Brewing Company Cookbook is very personal. You're looking into the thought processes, the stories behind the beers and what brought them into being. I don't get to see David as often as I would like. He's 800 miles from me, yet his warmth and commitment shine through on every page. The book challenges your expectations and offers new ideas in flavor combinations and inspirations. Sun Brewing is a product of its community and The Sun Brewing Company Cookbook is an insight about how David has integrated that community into his beers.

– BDB[2]
Bev D. Blackwood II
Editor
Southwest Brewing News

2

How to Read this Book.

How to Read this Book.

This book is for anyone who loves to get their hands a little dirty making great food and great beer. It's divided into four sections based on what you're looking for...

Readers who want to know who's behind these unusual recipes:

Start in Part One, where I narrate how I left my computer programming cubicle behind to become a YouTuber called El Guapo, the developer of the **borderlands avant-garde** culinary style, and the founder of Sun Brewing, El Paso's original craft brewery.

Readers who want to learn the borderlands avant-garde culinary philosophy:

In Part Two: Cooking with El Guapo, I give you a quick primer in how I approach all my recipe development so you can recreate the tastes of the borderland right in your own home.

Homebrewers:

Part Three: El Guapo's Brew Kettle, won't teach you how to homebrew (there are plenty of books and videos on that), but it will give beginning homebrewers the essential knowledge you'll need to avoid the mistakes I did. Then you can try out some of my borderland beers for yourself.

Keep reading in Part Three for more delicate and complicated beer recipes for advanced homebrewers, especially the sections on Borderland Avant-Garde Beers, 100% Spontaneous Ales, and my award-winning beer recipes.

Readers who enjoy cooking:

Part Four: El Guapo's Kitchen has something to inspire everyone. This section has beginner-level recipes in each section but also includes more advanced cooking methods such as working with fermented foods. I suggest Sun Brewing beers to pair with the food, and many recipes use Sun beers as ingredients (you're going to spend some time in Part Three), but I also suggest more readily available beers if you can't get your hands on a Sun beer.

Note: If substituting a Sun beer then use the same style. For example, IPA to IPA, Stout to Stout, Saison to Saison, 100% Spontaneous Ale to Belgian Lambic and so forth and so on.

3

Sundown on a Chapter in My Life.

Sundown on a Chapter in My Life.

When I was laid off from Hewlett Packard the first time, it threw me for a loop. A career in computers was Plans A through Z. If I couldn't do that, where did it leave me?

That night, I grabbed a few bottles of homebrew and lay down on a lounger in my back yard. My dogs, Boots and Camo, lay down next to me to keep me company. It was late at night, and my family and likely everyone else in the neighborhood was fast asleep. Above me, the big Texas sky spread out its majestic light show. I felt tiny and insignificant, and that felt good. I took comfort in knowing my problems were pretty small in the grand scheme of things.

I laid out there a long time, and then I laid out there some more. I was thinking about who I had been and who I was, now. Who did I want to be?

I was and will always be grateful to HP for the opportunities and experiences my position there offered me, like traveling around the country working for multimillion-dollar contracts for companies like the IRS and Coca-Cola. I'd found a kind of success, but something had always been missing in my life. I needed something more, to make a different kind of difference, if you will.

Eventually, the sun came up over the horizon, and I was still out there in the yard, nursing a beer. I'd been out there all night, and now it was sunup on a new day.

That's when it dawned on me (literally): The answer was right there in my hands. I'd been homebrewing for years just for fun and had gotten pretty good at it. I'd also been barbecuing and cooking every chance I had, developing my own recipes.

It would take a couple more years, but Sun Brewing was born that cool summer morning. The rest is the unfolding history of beer in El Paso. We were the only brewery in El Paso at that time and we were the first local brewery to distribute craft beer in the History of Beer in El Paso.

"You have to have a lot of passion for what you are doing because it is so hard… If you don't, any rational person would give up"
— Steve Jobs

Sun Brewing is a Revolutionary, International Award-Winning Brewery.

It was a serious risk, but I was in love. I was in love, and being in love is a risky business. It was also a calculated risk. I took the chance, but then I started researching to learn what it would take to make my vision a reality.

Take a look at this painting. It was done by local artist Ben Avant and depicts the back view of Sun Brewing and the Franklin Mountains. Ben recently passed away and was a very good friend of mine. RIP, friend.

Canutillo is filled with good people like Ben. You actually know the people running their businesses. A handshake and your word is all you need to do business in Canutillo. What I see in Canutillo is an older guy named Tury selling his locally farmed fruits and vegetables in the heart of Canutillo. This is beautiful to me. I see the flea market on the weekends and people going to the local grocery store owned by Victor, who you'll see running his business like a foot soldier on the front lines. I respect that.

Canutillo is a three-mile triangle in the far west side, upper valley of El Paso. What Canutillo is to El Paso, Texas, is what Old Mesilla is to Las Cruces, New Mexico. When I was scouting locations, I thought, "How beautiful would it be to set up a rustic brewery right on the Rio Grande in the center of the borderlands and tri-city area?"

Then it was time to be a doer. The doers are the real

thinkers. Through perseverance and grit, we can build our business one cement block at a time. Literally. I made my own cement and painted my own walls for my brewery and restaurant. We can rise and change the game. It's a passionate and intimate journey where we can evolve and keep climbing.

PART ONE: THE STORY OF SUN BREWING

5

Becoming El Guapo.

Ingredients.

I grew up on fried chicken and tamales! My father's family is from the Deep South, primarily Mississippi, Tennessee, Alabama, and Georgia. My mother's family had heavy influences from Mexican culture because my Grandma Julie was Mexican American and my Great-Grandma and Grandpa Cantu were Mexican. I had Southern cuisine from my dad's side and Mexican food from my mom's side. I always looked forward to the holidays, when we would have big family mealsOn Thanksgiving, Granny Slocum would make turkey and her traditional family stuffing while trying to watch M*A*S*H on TV. On Christmas, it was fried chicken! On Grandma Julie's side, the big food event at Christmastime was getting together at my Aunt CC's to make 100 tamales. All my grandma's sisters were there helping out. It was a beautiful thing of passing down family recipes and socializing. Everyone is socializing, having good times and learning, my grandma's sister, my aunt Elvira would talk to my mom and explain the process to her. My great grandma Cantu taught them all and now they are teaching my mom and my cousins. Some of my cousins even got the recipes. My cousin, Carolina, from Boston, now cooks everything from cottage cheese enchiladas to **migas** after the family style. She learned to cook Mexican food from the best —my Great Grandma Cantu.

My family's background had a profound influence on my love for both the familiarity of comfort food and the excitement of something new. Grandma Slocum made the best fried chicken I've tasted in all my life. Grandma Julie made the best mole on the planet. My mom remembers growing in up in Los Angeles and her mom taking her to see Great-Grandma Cantu's amazing tortillas— stacked so high you could barely see her eyes—and people also talked about her chicken feet soup. My dad was very traditional, but he was masterful at whatever he did in the kitchen or on the grill. My mom was an expert at creating new concoctions that nobody ever heard of but that always turned out great.

I remember fondly our big family gatherings at the park or in the yard, grilling out with a full house. Watching my family socialize, having ice cold beers and eating some home-cooked meals, was heaven on earth for me growing up. Good food and drink were themselves a social event in my family. They gave reason enough for the older generations to get together to share stories late into the night, sitting around the kitchen table or in lawn chairs in the back yard. Some of my best memories are of listening to them all laughing, debating, and sharing old stories—always with food and drink between them.

My love for barbecue originated from my dad. Usually, he made some kind of chicken or pork, but anything was fair game, including pheasant or duck. I'm telling you: My dad made the best BBQ chicken on earth! Second to none (and I'll fight you on that!). His technique was always low and slow and very tender. Sometimes, he would add some BBQ sauce, but it was never spicy—more sweet and tangy. He also loved lemon meringue, which was a flavor that took time to grow on me.

My dad had a tremendous impact on me, not only regarding barbecue but in major decisions I've made throughout my life. He served in the Marine Corps in the 60s, and after 9/11, I followed in his footsteps and joined up.

Being raised in a military family meant moving around my entire life every two years or less before we settled down in El Paso for my middle school and high school years. All that moving could be tough, but it also meant being injected into different cultures and experiencing their food and drinks. These were great life experiences for me and paved the way for me pursuing my brewery and restaurant. Traveling mesmerized me—seeing all the different people from all over the world, and especially enjoying their cuisines!

When I was in the Marines, I remember seeing what looked like tortillas and quesadillas in Afghanistan. I had also seen tortillas in Iraq with what looked to be Spanish rice. I distinctively remember telling my friends in Iraq that this place looks a lot like Mexico. People thought I was nuts, but I was being serious: the narrow streets and high street curbs and the building architecture all reminded me of Mexico.

I was convinced there was a connection, and I later learned I was correct. Spain fought in battles and wars with the Arabs over the centuries, which infused some of their cultures into each other. There is a wavy historical line connecting Iraq and Mexico. I have seen it not only in the food but in the domed architecture of both countries. The famous Mexican al Pastor tacos are from Middle Eastern heritage, most likely from Lebanese immigrants.

Food will always reveal how we are a lot more similar than what may appear on the surface. Every culture loves to eat, and they're generally happy to borrow from other cultures when they find something particularly tasty. One of my favorite Mexican sauces of all time is chamoy sauce. Chamoy sauce originated from China and over time became uniquely Mexican.

Becoming El Guapo.

I've always had admiration for business owners. As a young boy, I heard stories of my Great-Grandpa Cantu and how he bought equipment to make tortillas and started his own business. Growing up in the Deep South also had an impact on me, because everyone is self-sufficient in the South, even if it's a real small tobacco crop in the back yard. Everywhere you see, somebody has a business of some kind. It's definitely that way in Mexico, too; everywhere you look, little entrepreneurs try to make a living. To a certain extent, you can even see the same in El Paso.

Traveling is one of the greatest gifts the military can give someone. You see the entrepreneurial spirit of a great many different people even if it's on a street corner selling tea out of a wagon. Watching so many people around the world selling street food or working their business inspired me in a profound way. I watched in admiration and wanted to be like them: an entrepreneur.

In the Marines, I also noticed how a lot of veterans and former service members stayed near base and started businesses. That fateful night in my backyard, I remembered the mom-and-pop barbecue joint in 29 Palms, California, that I loved to go to when I had a little freedom from training. Same in Jacksonville, North Carolina—all kinds of veteran-led businesses.

Once I returned from Iraq, I got out of the Marines immediately. I extended for my last combat tour, and when I got home, I packed up and drove off Camp Lejeune in Jacksonville, North Carolina, for the last time. It was a surreal experience. One moment I'm with 1/6 "HARD" Infantry Battalion and the next I'm driving off base into the civilian world. I had saved a lot of money from back-to-back combat tours, so I started traveling to decompress a bit, hitting city after city down the east coast until I hit the farthest island I could find: Key West.

My cousin Joe was with me for that part. What a trip! I actually saw the chicken cross the road, and people can drink in the streets, there. In fact, we were drinking beers when we saw the chicken cross Duval Street.

Key West was a very unique experience. The food had Caribbean and Cuban influences blended with classic European cuisines, which I loved. We stopped at every little mom-and-pop shop we had room for. In one place, we had black beans and pork, and a guy pulled out a drill to make a hole in my coconut for a straw. I think I must have drunk at the world's smallest coffee shop, there. And, of course, the Key lime pie!

I eventually made it all the way to back to El Paso, Texas, where I had spent some important early years and had friends from childhood. I was kind of lost for a bit, wandering around, sitting under trees, sipping on my brew and just observing the birds and squirrels enjoying the simple things in life. Eventually, I started to adapt and think about getting a job outside the world's most famous gun club—The Marines.

I didn't stay in El Paso long. Before I had left the Marines, my friend Raul had suggested I move back to El Paso and invited me to stay with him. Raul and I had gone to high school together, and even after I left I often came back to town to visit him. By the time I got back after the Marines, however, Raul and his family had moved to Juarez, Mexico. I needed a job and a new start. As crazy as it sounds, I moved to Juarez to live with Raul and his family.

It wasn't as big of a leap as it would be for a lot of other gringos because I grew up in El Paso at a time when it was a rite of passage to cross the border as a teen in high school. I was the crazy guy always traveling throughout Mexico, heading to Ensenada for a drive down the coastline, stopping for burritos, or going to Durango to see a lifelong friend of mine get married.

I learned what it's like to be Mexican, at least a little bit. I lived in Mexico and experienced their culture and cuisines. As close as Juarez is to El Paso, they are worlds apart. Mexicans are very traditional. It's rare you see tattoos or lowriders;

those are uniquely Mexican-American things. Mexicans take their style very seriously—creases in their shirts and pants. I work with a lot of Mexican nationals who are engineers, and they are always the best dressed and are some of the very best engineers.

There are other differences that are more difficult to explain. For example, I know the Mexican food is better in Juarez than El Paso, though I can't articulate why. I just know it to be true for my taste buds.

One of the most striking aspects of Mexican culture is how warm it truly is. Mexicans will never skip the formalities. They will always greet you in the morning and say "Buenos dias" and ask how you are; they are extremely relationship based. A Mexican will normally not do business with you if they do not feel comfortable with you and like you. The social aspect is very important to them. You need to sit down and have good conversations and get to know them first. This is fascinating to me.

I was just some crazy jarhead Gringo who crossed the border every day and night to go back and forth to work. Locals on both sides couldn't believe it. I literally had lines of people waiting for me to cross the bridge to verify it was true. You learn things crossing the border; there are a lot of challenges, especially if you're a gringo. One important lesson was to never eat menudo or breakfast or drink liquids in the morning because you'll be in line waiting for hours and you do not want to poop yourself or pee yourself. You start adapting to your environment.

My first job out of the military was a minimum-wage gig

in a call center. I was the type of guy who would walk right into the highest manager's office and talk about myself just to network. Some people brushed me off and others listened to me, but I told them all, "Give me a chance, because I can do it. Just give a me a shot to show you what I can do." I kept hammering away, telling management that I was educated, with a bachelor's in computer science, and explaining what I could do for them. This paid dividends in the long run because I landed my first IT job as a technician and junior network admin in that same call center and kept climbing from there.

I eventually did a career change and took a job as a software engineer for Hewlett Packard. I really liked working for HP, traveling around the country to consult with clients as a high-level engineer. It was a lot of work, and when you're in front of clients, there's an exciting kind of pressure involved. Then came that first round of layoffs and my night of reflection under the stars and the realization that I was not in control of my own destiny.

When I was brought back to work, I told a colleague that I had this idea that was pretty crazy but I had decided to go for it. "I'm going to do it," I said. "I'm going to start my own brewery and restaurant."

He laughed at me.

And he kept laughing at me and looking at me funny as if waiting for me to break and tell him I was joking. Instead, I got a serious chip on my shoulder. I used it to motivate me to become great one day. I started to tell people I was going to make world-class beer. Maybe people laughed at me because El Paso didn't have a big craft beer scene, yet, and opening a brewery and restaurant is associated with having a lot of money to invest. I could never really figure out all the reasons people laughed at me, but one thing was for certain: I was determined to build my own brewery with my own two hands.

The day I won my first gold medal, I had tears in my eyes. Then there were more medals. Becoming a multiple international award-winning brewer and brewery has a way of validating a guy's crazy ideas.

"Those who are crazy enough to think they can change the world usually do." — Steve Jobs

All of these experiences shaped me. I really loved living in Juarez and traveling throughout Mexico, experimenting with the different cuisines in each region. This is where my love for street food matured to an entire new level. Juarez is the Mecca of street food, and this city is where my love for **tripitas**, **machitos**, and **tepache** took off.

Naturally, I would drink Mexican beer with street food, and my favorite of all Mexican beers was Dos Equis Amber, which is a Mexican-style Vienna lager. It wasn't long before I started to try to emulate what I was tasting. Then I started trying to make food like what I was eating on the street.

It was never on my radar to make "great beer." It was more a question of whether I could make decent beer, beer that I could enjoy drinking and appreciate was my own. To some extent, I was very late in the game of home brewing. I wasn't accomplished and I didn't have any mentors. I brewed to drink my own beer with no expectations of being world class. Pretty much the same went for all my food, too; I wanted to cook family recipes good enough to enjoy.

When I decided to turn my hobby into a career, there was no question that I would also have a restaurant. I brewed beer inspired by different foods, and I cooked with my beer. They went together. But before I opened, I felt I needed a movie-star name for my future Hollywood Sun Brewing star (why I thought becoming a brewer was in any way connected to getting a star, I don't know; it's not really important). So, I became Brewmaster and Chef David "El Guapo" Slocum.

El Guapo translates as something like The Handsome Male. I thought it was comical, but not in a bad way, and whoever has this name would have to have a sense of humor and to be bold. Famous people have used the nickname, too, like the mixed martial artist Bas Rutten. I thought it was so funny seeing Bas on TV referring to himself as El Guapo when he was smack-talking his opponent. I also thought it would be a funny reference to *The Three Amigos*. "Would you say I have a *plethora* of cervezas?"

I ended up doing great things and had a lot of fun as El Guapo. Perhaps the most fun is my YouTube channel, called "Cooking with El Guapo." I hope it inspires others. Surely, there are many other El Guapos out there who embody the spirit of brewing and cooking; they just haven't been seen or discovered or started their own business, yet. Hopefully, one day I'll see legions of El Guapos (and La Guapas) out there brewing world-class beer out of a bucket for street beer or a brewpub. It doesn't matter the size of the brewery, just that you're doing it.

Back in them days, as a young El Guapo, I was just a professional homebrewer and backyard cook goofing off and having a lot of fun. El Guapo, the character, was somewhat of a stand-up comedian cooking food and brewing beer. I didn't take myself too seriously... I was just having fun and experimenting and trying to show people that it's a lot of fun cooking and brewing. I started a cooking show when there was nothing of its kind in all of El Paso, yet, though I didn't appreciate that it would be so revolutionary.

Nobody in all of El Paso was cooking with beer, and there was certainly no brewing scene. As time passed, I discovered that I actually did want to become a world-class brewer, stunning the world with my magnificent beer. I wanted to make the very best beer in the entire world.

It's funny how life works, I went from the Marines to gypsy nomad traveler to a Gringo-Mexican crossing the bridge every day to an IT professional to an entertainer/entrepreneur with my own cooking show, being a free spirit, brewing and cooking with beer. It was good times. I did approximately 24 episodes in two years, but I slowed down dramatically after the birth of my son, Jake Andres "El Guapito" Slocum. For a couple years, instead of making episodes I was changing diapers and being with my son. One of life's greatest joy's is changing diapers!

I hope to instill in my kids, Natalie, Anita, and Jake, that life is too short, so you need to go for it, whatever it is! Follow your dreams because it's worth the risk to go off on your own with the chance of being truly happy.

Everything Under the Sun.

The name of the brewery came easy to me because El Paso is the Sun City and I was laying outside under the stars when I dreamed up the concept—the sun is a star, after all. The sun is also an ancient ingredient for the first beers made on earth. The name seemed a perfect fit that was simple and matched the concept of my brewpub.

Sun Brewing embodies my hybrid culinary style, which I call Borderland Avant-garde—indigenous beers and foods infused with local flavors to create something unique to the region. I didn't want to perfect the same pale ale but to create beers that the world has never seen before. This complemented my goals of an intimate and unique atmosphere. My slogan since day one has been, "There is nothing more intimate than crafting something homemade from someone's hands to another's."

The borderland avant-garde style of beer features ingredients like hibiscus, Mexican chocolate and New Mexican chile peppers. As you'll see in Part Four, this fusion creates unique and exciting dishes like my 6th Anniversary Tamales, Fermented Chile Fried Chicken, and 100% Spontaneous Breads.

It sounds crazy because I was going to do something that didn't have a name until I gave it one, with no formal training or background. Even though the odds were dramatically stacked against me (or anyone in my position), nothing was going to stop me from at least trying to make my dreams into a reality. I had made up my mind and was going full speed ahead to carry this out to the very end. I remember making it to the finish line on opening day, and the feeling was indescribable. All the hard work and all the dreams had become a reality.

My grand opening was July 5th, 2014. After all those months of planning and building, I'd made it! I was paying rent for over half a year before I opened, and I'd been working on Sun Brewing for a good half year before that. It was my first business, and on the day I first opened my doors to customers I teared up. I was so happy that I made it to the finish line and was actually living my dream.

In those first days, weeks, and months of Sun Brewing, the overwhelming majority of my customers didn't even know what craft beer was, not to mention borderland avant-garde beer. With nearly every customer, I had to have a little conversation about what craft beer means to me and what I believe craft beer really is. A lot of people would tell me how they just bought a quart of some craft beer called Sol—people were confusing imports with craft beer. It wasn't their fault; beer commercials from beer giants were calling their beer craft on the radio at the time. There was a lot of confusion over what craft beer really is; it always made for great conversations.

I was the only operational brewery in all of El Paso at that time, and when people would stop by, they would think I was brewing coffee or tea. When I told them I was brewing beer, they all looked shocked. It was more difficult because my beer wasn't exactly standard. I was trying to sell my Meados de Alien [Alien Piss], which had apricots and New Mexican chiles in it, to people who drank commercial Mexican lagers. People thought I was nuts; maybe I was. The other beer I was making was a Mexican-chocolate spiced porter.

El Guapo never shied away from a challenge.

I dreamed up a story of a journey through the desert mountains, and I wrote a short story and made it into a short film for an advertisement. At that point in time, I didn't have the money for big time commercials, so I used social media to promote my short films of the messages I wanted to convey to the public. You can still find them on YouTube:

https://www.youtube.com/watch?v=hCu7p8l2MtU

https://www.youtube.com/watch?v=dmnXJONIPcA

At the end of the day, flavor and quality always win out. In order to pull off what I wanted to do, I really needed to have a beer that people loved. Meados de Alien did exactly that. People loved my Meados, and that paved the way for the rest of my borderland avant-garde style of beers. If I could get people to try it, they always loved it. I believed it was just a matter of time before people would really embrace my beers because they tasted good and were unique.

"It's better to fail in Originality than succeed in Imitation" — Herman Melville

Brewing beer and cooking food is how I express myself. It's very romantic to create your own food and drink. I love creating original beer and food concoctions; it gives me the same feeling I had in college building my first computer or creating my first video game. The feeling of creating something is intoxicating and very addicting. It's giving an intimate part of yourself to others.

I was considered weird brewing beers with my unique

ingredients. Newcomers to craft couldn't understand my flavors, and traditionalists thought I was committing a sin. But I'm okay with weird. I knew my beer could be world class, though I also knew it was going to take a lot of hard work and process improvements over time. Good beer is good beer regardless of the size of the brewery or our definitions of what a beer is. Nowadays, nobody has an issue with weird beers; I've created a new normal.

The beautiful artistry of creating my own borderland avant-garde beer comes from my dreams and my imagination. I believe we all have the ability and opportunity to make our dreams a reality. I built Sun Brewing with my own vision, and you can build something with your own, too.

Where there is a will, there is a way. Whether it's dreaming up your next revolutionary beer or building a loft with your own hands, brick by brick, we can rise and change the game. It's a journey of passion where we can evolve and keep climbing.

There is always a way.

Sun Brewing is proof of that.

6

PART TWO: COOKING WITH EL GUAPO

7

Cooking with Beer.

There's No Such Thing as a Recipe.

Maybe it's not a bright idea to include a chapter in your cookbook called "There's No Such Thing as a Recipe," but you're cooking with El Guapo, now. Yes, there are recipes in this book, but they're more guidelines than formulas.

When it comes to cooking, there are of course factors and variables that affect your results, ranging from variations in water profiles to the size and strength of your own hands. But there is no *exact* recipe. What we can do is feel, see, taste, and know when to adjust.

We have our own natural, innate senses for cooking and brewing. Most people, given the right tools, could become master technicians. The real beauty in brewing and cooking, however, is relying on your own taste buds to create new flavors that are all your own.

Some people don't like *this* and others love *that*. What is it that you love? Do you love hibiscus water? Do you not like cinnamon spice? What is your flavor? What you love is within you... All too often people are told (or hear) that this is right and this is wrong in brewing and cooking.

The First Principle: What You Love is Right

El Guapo's philosophy? *What you love is what is right.*

Write that on the front of all your cookbooks to remind you that *you* are the cook, *you* get to play in the kitchen and make the rules.

Bring out what you love and make it happen. It may not be the greatest at first try, but that's okay because you know what flavors you love. It's just a matter of finding the right combinations!

I say, if it tastes great, it's right, and if it stinks, it's wrong.

Take, for example, Mexican mole's two basic ingredients: Mexican chocolate and chiles. These are two very different, contrasting flavors—but they're absolutely magnificent together! Another example is steak and oyster stew! Oysters in a thick, hearty steak stew? Who knew that would work? Or better yet, in a stout! Thick, hearty, steak and oyster pie!

Oysters and steak: What a combination! Oyster stout: What a concept!

The world, as they say, is your oyster.

I consider my cuisine fusion, but really we are all a fusion to a certain extent, and our cuisines are cultures of cultures. A lot of my food is based off Southern food and Mexican food because that's my background. You have your own cultural backgrounds to draw from. What would a Turkish-Czech dish look like? Or Chinese Tex-Mex?

My borderland avant-garde style of beer is inspired by borderlands, tri-city regional flavors (El Paso-Juarez-Las Cruces). This fusion is difficult on many levels because it's truly breaking the norms and creating new normals. I have to think outside of the box, but also find ways to make the food approachable to people who have never heard of it before.

Here's a little secret: "approachable" isn't so hard when the food looks and smells great. We eat with our eyes, after all.

The Second Principle: Trust Your Crazy

To cook with El Guapo, you have to follow what interests you, even if—especially if—it takes you out of your comfort zone and into crazy town.

When I create something new but unexpected and just love it, I ask myself: Is this dish or beer crazy? Is it delusional? Is it magnificent? If I tell myself yes to any of these (especially the last one), then I know I'm on the right track.

A good example is when I came up with the Tripitas Dog. The Tripitas Dog is a Sun Brewing original; to my knowledge, it's never been done before. It's an All-American hot dog boiled in beer, then made into a splitter dog, grilled, and topped with tripitas, diced onions, salsa, and cilantro. Two different foods from two different cultures in fusion.

It's a very simple idea that comes from my personal experiences and tastes, but because tripitas are not part of the vocabulary of the average American palate, it's definitely in the crazy camp.

But who don't love a good dog? It's an American classic, and the Tripitas Dog is my way of expanding American tastes, combining something we all love with something that's new for a lot of people.

Tepache is a fantastic borderlands beverage!

I make traditional tepache, but I also make several different beers of tepache. To my knowledge, I was the first to ever make a beer with actual tepache in it. Certainly the first to sell it. Imagine the citrus and tropical hops of a beer fused with the beautiful pineapple and spice flavors of traditional tepache... magnificent!

I'm very proud to have done this, and I love serving it to customers. It's a very unique beverage tasting of sour and spice; there is nothing quite like it. Few people in El Paso even knew what tepache was, despite being so close to Juarez (I told you, they're different worlds), but I'm proud to have contributed to its growing popularity.

The Third Principle: Your Hands are for Giving Gifts

This is part of the wonder of brewing and cooking. To me, there is nothing more satisfying than making something nobody has heard of and seeing the look on their faces (and hearing the satisfied sounds) when they first try it.

Philosophically, I love the idea of cooking something in my little kitchen and serving it to other people. It's as special and intimate as a person can get with the Sun Brewing experience. What I make with my hands I can give as a gift to you.

That's a huge value for me as a restaurateur: The person who cooks the food also serves it.

What a concept! I love it! Whoever cooks food in my little kitchen also serves it. My good friend and one of my cooks, Chino, doesn't really look the part of a hip cook, but he makes some spectacular dishes. And then he brings the food out. We all cook, and we all serve what we cook to our customers. It creates a personal connection from our hands straight to yours.

This is the main reason for having a kitchen with a brewery in the first place, as far as I'm concerned. The brewery experience is amplified through the intimacy of our food and beer pairings served by the same hands that made it.

The same goes at home. Embrace the experience of cooking as a personal, intimate gift you can give to your family and guests. You're doing something special every time you chop a carrot or throw meat on a grill.

"Context and memory play powerful roles in all the truly great meals in one's life"
— Anthony Bourdain

The Fourth Principle: You Can Always Make It Again

Brewing and cooking something intimate and special takes a lot of fine tuning and small incremental process improvements over time. If a dish or beer doesn't turn out right, it doesn't mean you're bad at this stuff. Maybe you can still serve it, or maybe you have to toss it, but look, you can always make it again. You'll just have to make it different next time.

When you design a recipe, you will have to make many adjustments until you are satisfied. When I first designed the recipe to Meados de Alien, I initially dumped sugar into the fermentation straight up without purifying it. This made me vulnerable to contamination. Sometimes the beer would turn out fantastic and other times not so much. It was hit or miss. When it was a hit, it was huge with the people. When it was a miss, I was out the cost of ingredients, the time, and the opportunity to sell more Meados.

I soon learned that I needed to boil the sugar before dumping it into the fermentation. Problem solved. Every beer I've ever made has a history of tweaking the recipe. Every dish I've ever made needed improvements, especially at the beginning. Often, I was trying to achieve balance, but sometimes I was trying to accentuate a certain flavor—for example, a sour flavor or a bitter flavor. Even if I wanted to bring out a certain flavor, I wanted it romantic and not harsh. It took time.

Sometimes, your accidents will turn into colossal success stories. Take, for example, my Descalzo Hybrid Ale. The original hybrid beer I made was called Frankenstein because I used wine yeast in Syrah grape must from a local vineyard. The following year, they didn't have Syrah grape must, so they gave me a blend of pinot grigio grape must. I used that grape must in the fermentation and created one of the greatest tasting hybrid ales I've ever made. People went nuts over it, especially if they were into dry slightly fruity white wines. What I thought was a potential disaster for that brand turned out to be a success.

Even your failures can turn into successes. Back when I first brewed a porter, it didn't turn out the way I wanted it. It wasn't a failure in the sense of being bad beer, but it was a failure in the sense of achieving my vision. I kept trying, tweaking and playing with it and with my stout recipe; these can be very nuanced because of the strength of the roasted malts.

At the time, I had a secret habit of squirting a lime into my pints of porter. I didn't tell anyone at first because people already thought my beers were weird. But then I followed the El Guapo philosophy:

Did I love it? Yes.

Was it crazy? Yes.

Was it magnificent? Undoubtedly.

Eventually, I created the recipes for Fozzie Lime Stout and

Symposius Sour Porter. Symposius Sour Porter is one of my favorites; the sourness contrasts with the roasted grains of the malt. For the Fozzie Lime Stout, think of it like squeezing lime on your elote or your fajitas and it won't seem so weird. The Fozzie is good, but you'll want a slight undertone from the limes. I've also used lemons in porters and liked it. A little experimentation led to the birth of a delightful new flavor profile within the porter and stout base style. Everything has value and we build off of every single thing we do as brewers..

You're going to have successes and failures and sometimes your mistakes turn out to be great. I've failed a great many times, but when I did, I failed magnificently. Once you've failed enough, then you will change your outlook on what failure means. I started to actually like my failures until the line between a failure and a success became kind of hazy. In all failures is the chance to learn something that eventually leads to success.

You just need to make it again.

You, Too, Can Learn to Cook with Beer.

Beer is not only for drinking but also for cooking. Cooking with beer is truly magnificent! It's magnificent because of all the unique complexities it brings to the dish. Beer adds complexity to food by its fusion with everything, from emulsifying sauces, baking breads, preparing desserts, barbecuing, and everything else in between.

I think beer enhances food in wonderful ways. The infinite

combinations of beers and foods offer layers of complexity. Beer infuses itself with your food to give the dish unique flavors.

Take, for example, the Maillard reaction, which is the chemical reaction between amino acids and sugar reduction that gives distinct flavors from the browning of foods. Examples of the Maillard reaction are roasted marshmallows, the crust of baked breads, and seared meats. This adds incredible flavors to foods, including beer! Imagine a stout burger or stout caramelized onions!!

Caramelization is slightly different than the Maillard reaction because caramelization involves only the chemical reactions from heating sugars. Onions are naturally sweet and when heated caramelize, but imagine a stout combined with an onion to create a stout onion marmalade! The possibilities are endless: How about a 100% spontaneous-beer bread crusted to perfection or a seared beer burger?

As you've probably guessed, I love cooking with stout.

"He was a wise man who invented beer." — Plato

How I choose beer for cooking.

To learn how to cook with beer, it's worth reviewing the basic taste buds first.

1. *Sweet* — This is basically our response to sugar, our "sweet tooth."
2. *Salty* — Table salt (NaCl) is a taste enhancer.
3. *Sour* — We think of citrus, but chemically, this registers the presence of acids.

4. *Bitter* — The corollary of sour, this taste is the presence of bases. Bitterness can be harsh at times if used in excess or cooked in a certain way, however bitterness can have an exquisite taste!

A bitter beer example would be the American IPA, which has taken over the world with its elegant bitter taste. Unsweetened chocolate is another bitter taste; we usually combine chocolate with something sweet. Bitter flavors are almost always balanced in some form with other flavors and usually with some level of sweetness. Citrus peels have a strong bitter taste but are great for cooking and brewing. Lemon zest and orange zest are used in a wide array of beers and food dishes.

Bitterness in my view is an acquired taste. IPAs are continuously gaining popularity in part because people's tastes are changing over time. A lot of people are not accustomed to bitter flavors, but when you have a great tasting bitter flavor it can open up a new world of possibilities for flavorful beer and food combinations.

There is still a lot to be explored, learned, and created in this taste category.
5. *Umami* — This is also known as savory. Umami is basically a (delicious) hearty and meaty flavor.

If they ever discover a sixth taste bud, I predict it will be specifically for fried chicken. That, or true Mexican **carnitas**!

They're one of my favorites and remind me of some cross between chicken feet and **chicharrones** layered over the mixed pig parts.

Recipe creation is basically a matter of how you combine these taste categories. Here is a basic guide for pairing beer and food. This works for both cooking with beer and serving a cold beer with your dish.

Note: My most fundamental approach for choosing a beer to cook with is, "If it pairs well, then it should cook well." The following are only cookie cutter rules of thumb but they are a good place to start.

Complement

This is the most basic approach: pairing like to like. For example, sweet to sweet or sour to sour.

This could be a beer float of porter and chocolate ice cream. The classic approach is a porter with vanilla ice cream, but porter has rich roasty, chocolaty, and sweet flavors and thus pairs well with chocolate.

Vanilla ice cream is sweet from the sugar and complex from the vanilla. Vanilla has a beautiful aroma that's woody, smoky, and sweet and enhances the sweet, fruity, and rich flavors.

You could also do a porter beer reduction and use it as a topping for the vanilla ice cream to make a dessert. You could dress this up with several combinations of spice, nuts, and chocolate.

Or pair a malt-forward beer like an English mild or brown ale with gouda cheese. Malt-forward beers are sweet with notes of nuts, caramel, and toffee flavors that can really complement the rich nutty flavors of some cheeses.

My favorite is to pair malty beers with barbecue. A slow-cooked medium-rare prime rib goes great with a brown ale. The roasted and caramel undertones of the beer complement the charred savory sweetness of the steak.

Contrast

Contrasting pairs different taste buds. For example, sweet-and-sour sauce mixes guava and red jalapenos. Guava is high in sugar, and the acidity of the peppers balances it by cutting through the sweetness. You can make a spiced sweet-and-sour beer sauce with a sour ale, guava, and peppers.

The absolute greatest sauce in the history of sauces (for contrasting flavors) is **chamoy** sauce! It's my favorite! I love it so much that I made a chamoy beer. Chamoy sauce is made with fruit and chiles, like a Mexican sweet-and-sour sauce.

Here's a mind-bender: Make a beer float with sour beer and guava ice cream. You could also pair a sour saison with a banana split.

Or you could make a sour saison ice cream. The acidity from the sour beer is strong and the ice cream has a pronounced sweet taste. The complex flavors of the saison and the spice from the beer enhance and balance the sweetness of the ice cream.

Cleanse

This approach basically aims to balance strong flavors. For example, balancing hot wings with a Pilsner lager. Hot wings have a strong flavor. The Pilsner lager with its neutral flavor cleanses the palate from the strong flavor of the hot wings.

This can be tricky because there is a lot going on here. The hot sauce has vinegar in it, which is acidic. The peppers are added for spice and heat. Peppers are acidic for the most part, but peppers like cayenne are alkaline, which balances well with vinegar.

Cleansing the palate can work in many different ways. For example, you might want to cleanse the bitterness of an American IPA. You could use fried chicken, something similar to KFC's original. The fattiness (umami) cuts through the bitterness to balance it all out.

Another good option is to use amber ales for cleansing because of the dry and crisp finish. Caribbean jerk chicken pairs great with an American amber ale. I frequently use amber ales for my beer chicken barbecues. This is an excellent way to cook with beer.

My recommendation is to use your intuition. When in doubt, start by pairing a beer you think will be excellent for a dish. If it tastes good to drink the one and eat the other, then you hit the jack pot! Next time you're cooking that dish, throw a dash of that beer in there. For example, if I like to eat a classic lamb stew while drinking a stout, then I would experiment with making a stout lamb stew.

If the beer you choose doesn't work with that dish, then

the worst thing that happened was you had a good meal and a nice beer. Keep experimenting! In general, I do things to taste, but do not exclude possibilities of styles of beer you do not like. I experiment endlessly, especially after I've had a beer or two. That loosens me up to go straight to the kitchen and start playing!

Keep in mind these are rules of thumb and not law (there's no such thing as a recipe!). You do you, and if you like it, then it has to be right.

This does not mean I wouldn't cook food with beers I wouldn't normally pair with a dish. I play around. For instance, I threw my Frankenstein hybrid ale into a lamb stew. The flavors contrasted and it worked great.

Cooking with beer can be tricky at times; it can take a lot of experimentation. There have been many of times I made something with a striking beer like a sour or an IPA that wasn't the greatest. But I made it again—with a different beer. Once, I made beer bread with an extremely bitter IPA. The cooking process made the bread much too harsh. The same bread recipe with a New England IPA was pleasant and delightful.

So, keep at it. You're going to have to be Dr. Frankenstein in the kitchen, but that's what makes it all fun.

8

PART THREE: EL GUAPO'S BREW KETTLE

9

BAG Beers.

Beer Brewing Tips & Procedures.

Essentially, Sun Brewing is homebrew gone professional. Homebrewing legend Charlie Papazian once said, "Remember, the best beer in the world is the one you brewed." I'm proud to support and promote anyone who is a member of the American Homebrewers Association. Great brewers started in the home and make some of the best beers in the entire world. I like to think of myself as an ambitious homebrewer that is blissfully inefficient.

Note: I'm placing the beer recipes before the food because many of these beers will be ingredients for the food. I will also suggest beer alternatives for those of you who aren't homebrewers. But really, what's to lose by giving it a shot?

Beer Basics

Beer is a fermented beverage made from four basic ingredients:

1. **Barley** — A centuries-old grain, also known as *Hordeum vulgare* for barley geeks who malt their own.

    Barley must be malted so the yeast can convert to alcohol. Malting is essentially steeping grains in water until it begins to germinate.

    The type of malt you use helps provides the color and body of a beer. There are hundreds of different types of malt that provide different flavor profiles and millions of combinations.

2. **Water** — This is an extremely important aspect of beer. Beer is at least 90 percent water.

    I wouldn't go as far as to say that it's *the* most important aspect of beer because you can't have beer without other important ingredients. However, water is the easiest ingredient to take for granted or to underestimate.

3. **Hops** — Hops are the spice of beer; they add bitterness, flavor, and aroma. Hops can be added at any time during brewing, but we generally think in terms of the purpose for which we are adding them.

Hops added to the beginning of the boil are for *bittering*. We tend to choose hops that are high in alpha acids, which break down and isomerize with enough heat over time. Isomerization is a process by which one molecule is transformed into another molecule with the exact same atoms in a different arrangement. Isomerization of hops essentially brings out the hop character by making it soluble in the beer.

Bitterness is measured in international bitterness units (IBUs). Some beers have very little IBUs, like Pilsner lagers, while others have extreme amounts of bitterness like IPAs.

Flavoring hops are added at some point typically in between the last 15 minutes to the last 5 minutes of the boil. The reason for this is because the flavor characteristics of hops evaporate over a long boil. In order to preserve the flavoring component of your hops, you'll want to add them towards the end of the boil.

Aroma hops are added in the last 5 minutes of the boil. Two or three minutes is an ideal range for preserving the hops' aroma potential.

Dry hopping (hopping after the boil) is the best method

for adding aroma and flavor (aroma and flavor are intertwined). Dry hopping allows for maximum hop aroma and flavor in your beer. Typically, dry hopping is done in the last few days of fermentation or when fermentation is complete. Normally, you'll want to dry hop for at least three days and in some cases even a week or longer.
4. **Yeast** — The "soul of beer." Yeast gives us alcohol and bubblies in our beer. The truly divine part of it all...

Millions of yeast cells gobble up sugars from the wort (the sweet honey like substance from the mash) to produce a flavor symphony over a period of weeks and sometimes months and even years!

Saccharomyces cerevisiae is the top-fermenting yeast also known as ale yeast. If you've ever done an open fermentation, then you'll have seen a thick yeast cake on top of the wort with all the bubblies popping. This yeast produces fuller, more pronounced flavors, often with fruity and spicy esters.

Saccharomyces carlsbergensis is a bottom-fermenting yeast also known as lager yeast. Lager yeast fermentations are done at colder temperatures and typically have a neutral flavor. They are very clean and crisp tasting because very few esters are produced.

Wild yeasts are microorganisms that infect the wort from the air along with bacteria. These wild things can produce some of most complex and best-tasting beers the world has ever known. Spontaneous ales take years to make and are like a fine wine... they just get better with age.

Playing with Water

Water can be hard to get right as a homebrewer with limited facilities; most homebrewers don't have a lab, for instance. But have no fear! Where there is a will, there is a way!

There are a few ways I tackle the water issue in brewing. In order to have some sense of what we're doing, though, let's learn you some water knowledge. First, you'll want to pull your city's water report. Often, this can be found online, but if not, give them a call to see how you can get the numbers you want.

El Paso's Upper Valley Water Report, 2019

Ca	Mg	Na	Cl	SO_4	$CaCO_3$	pH
42	5.5	168	117	189	121	8.1

Here are the relevant numbers from the City of El Paso Chemical Analysis of City Water, Upper Valley, for 2019:

This may not make much sense to you, yet, but don't worry. Here are a few quick definitions:

pH — A measure of relative acidity and basicity in water. pH measures molar concentration of hydrogen ions in solution. The more hydrogen, the higher the pH, meaning the more basic or alkaline. A good starting water pH is around 7 to 8. Note that it's *the pH in your mash* that matters most. Adding grains can affect the pH.

water hardness — A description of the total magnesium and calcium in water (represented by Ca and Mg ions in the water report).

temporary hardness — The presence of dissolved carbonates and bicarbonates of calcium and magnesium. This is represented by alkalinity. Temporary hardness is not as important as water hardness because it is boiled out of the water. Boiling water precipitates out $CaCO_3$ as bicarbonate (HCO_3). You can measure temporary hardness by comparing the hardness of water before and after boiling.

sulfates — SO_4 in your water report. Most municipalities will have numbers lower than 50. Sulfates increase water hardness and aid in starch conversion in the mash. Sulfates enhance hop bitterness. The famous Burton-on-Trent water profile has an SO_4 of 720 ppm.

El Paso water is great for brewing because it is mineral-rich hard water. Malt-forward beers taste great because of El Paso's carbonate levels ($CaCO_3$), while bitter beers like black IPAs work well due to the sulfate levels (SO_4).

You can adjust your local water to your style needs, whether a soft water pale or a hard water roasted malty dark beer. Carbonates raise the pH and balance the acidity from darker grains. Sulfates accentuate bitterness in beer, which is good for IPAs.

Achieving an IPA Water Profile.

As great as El Paso's water is because of its rich mineral content, we still have to convert it to an ideal IPA water profile. There are two ways I tackle this problem.

The first way is to dilute the local water with purified water. You should really pull the water report for your bottled water. A lot of companies publish their water report online, but if they do not, then you can call them for it.

This involves some math. Say you're making a 50 percent / 50 percent dilution, for example. Since most local water supplies will be high in $CaCO_3$ and most purified water counts quite low, a 50/50 dilution is a good general-purpose water profile for any beer that you brew. If your target is a total of 5 gallons, then you would only use 2.5 gallons of local water and 2.5 gallons of purified water. This will not necessarily dilute your ions by half because you have to take into account what minerals are in the purified water. If the purified water's $CaCO_3$ ion count is 12 and your local water is 124, and you want a $CaCO_3$ of about 60, then you'll have to do a little algebra.

Or, you could do what a lot of homebrewers do and get yourself a brewing water calculator (there's a great one, as well as other recipe resources, at Brewersfriend.com. John Palmer has it all mapped out on his website, too).

When you get really technical, you will want to know the brewing range for each ion for each style of beer. An alkalinity of 60 is in the brewing range for amber ale. Again, there are charts online for brewing ranges. For beginners, you can focus on your alkalinity ($CaCO_3$).

If I wanted to dilute my local water for an IPA style, then I would need to dilute around 75 percent to get my carbonates to the 30 mg/L range. You can calculate where you want it within the standard IPA range. Once you have diluted your water and you have your new ion counts, then you'll need to add brewing salts to bring the calcium and sulfate levels back up. Calcium increases water hardness and aids in mash conversion. Sulfates accentuate bitterness, which is what we are targeting in this water profile.

We want our calcium to exceed our carbonate levels; we want low carbonates and higher calcium. For our 5-gallon batch, we brought the calcium levels of our El Paso water down to around 5 and our magnesium to around 47.

We use calcium sulfate (gypsum) to bring the levels back up. One gram per gallon of gypsum adds 62 ppm of calcium and 147 ppm of sulfate. If we added 5 grams (about 1 tsp) of gypsum to our batch, we'd get the Ca up to around 72. I like it a little higher, so I'll add 7.5 g (about 1.5 tsp) to bring my level to around 103 ppm Ca and over 220 ppm SO_4.

What we achieved was lowering the carbonates to our targeted carbonate levels and raising our calcium and sulfate levels.

There are different kinds of bitterness with respect to water. The first kind of bitterness is an extreme harshness and the other bitterness is romancing the hop flavors and aromas. This IPA profile brings out hop flavor but not in a harsh way.

Note: mg/L is equivalent to ppm when dealing with your water report.

The second way is to begin with purified water and build your water profile with brewing salts. I'll also use a combination with mineral water at times because I love a mineral water taste with certain beer styles such as a saison.

Reverse osmosis water also eliminates other impurities in the water. The other added benefit is consistency. You can make the same water every single time. The city water can vary at times over the years.

Basically, you'll really only need to use gypsum ($CaSO_4$) and calcium chloride (CaCl). You can buy this at your local homebrew store. It should also have instructions but if it doesn't, then you would use 1 tsp per 5 gallons in general for a standard water profile.

Let's take a look at building an IPA water profile.

You would use:

1 tsp calcium chloride

1 tsp of gypsum

Note: For an American Lager it would be very similar to the IPA water profile. I would use:

1 ½ tsp calcium chloride and 1 tsp of gypsum with 2 percent acid malt

Also Note: It's your water profile and its okay to design yours using higher chloride for an IPA like a pilsner would have especially if you're designing a NEIPA. New England IPA's have a higher chloride to sulphate ratio than a West Coast IPA. I make a West Coast IPA with a 1:3 ratio where a NEIPA would have a 3:1 ratio of a chloride to sulphate. Targeting 75 ppm chloride to 225 ppm sulphate.

I've never gone over 10 percent with acid malt. Basically, 1 percent of acid malt will reduce the pH by 0.1 percent. If you were to use 10 percent acid malt, then it would reduce your pH one full percentage point. For example, if you had a 6.3 pH it would reduce your pH to 5.3, which is the optimum pH value for your mash. The pH value outside of the mash is less important, but it's extremely important having a mash between 5.2 to 5.6.

You can measure your pH to be sure that it's in the 5.2 to 5.6 range for brewing. There are tools at your local home-brewing store to measure pH and normally if you have a good recipe then you'll hit your pH range from your grain bill.

Note: In general, use 1 to 3 percent acidulated malt, depending on your recipe: 3 percent with little to no specialty malts and 1 percent with some crystal malts.

If there is no acid malt, then you could use lactic acid to adjust the mash pH by adding it to the mash. I've also lowered the mash pH using lemon juice. Your local home brewing store should at least have one or the other. You'll want to start with just one teaspoon and take another reading. One teaspoon should lower the pH about half a point, though this varies depending on your mash. The new reading will be your benchmark and let you know how much more you may need to add.

Note: For dark beers like porters there is no need for acidulated malt because roasted grains are more acidic and lower mash pH.

Note: You are adding the brewing salts because of the calcium deficit from the dilution or distillation.

Chlorophenols in water.

There are issues with chlorophenols in your local tap water, too, that can be troublesome for brewing. Too much chlorophenols make beer taste and smell medicinal. If you don't have a water filter system, then you can boil the water to get most of the chlorophenols out. However, boiling will not take out chloramine; you can use a Camden tablet for this.

Cleaning and Sanitization Tips.

Cleaning and sanitization are key parts of brewing and about the only thing worth being really persnickety about. Keep in mind that not all cleaning is equal:

Clean — to get rid of everything on the surface area including stains

Sanitize — is to kill contaminating microorganisms and bacteria to negligible levels

Sterilize — is to kill all living microorganisms and bacteria

For brewing, we're generally satisfied with sanitization rather than full-on sterilization.

Some of the off flavors that I've had in my beer came from what sanitizer I chose to use. For example, I would use bleach and think that I rinsed thoroughly enough with hot water to wash all the bleach away. I was wrong and ruined several batches of beer this way.

My advice is to *stay away from bleach* because a minuscule amount of bleach will ruin your beer. Always use Star San or an equivalent for sanitizing.

For cleaning you can use PBW cleaner or TSP (Trisodium phosphate). The benefit to TSP is you can use small amounts of it to clean your equipment and it's cost effective. PBW is the best all-purpose cleaner. Star San is an acidic sanitizer; it's the best sanitizer for brewing on the market and will not contribute to off flavors.

For bottling, you are going to want to buy a bottle brush and clean each and every bottle with PBW and rinse it thoroughly. Sanitize with Star San for at least 5 minutes. Use this same process for all your brewing equipment.

For kegs, it's the same as cleaning bottles. You will want to use a brush to clean the inside of the keg thoroughly with PBW followed by sanitizing with Star San.

For the 7.5-gallon stainless steel fermenters, you will need to disassemble, clean, and sanitize each and every individual part. Then you'll want to reassemble the fermenter and sanitize it again with Star San.

There are all kinds of different methods for cleaning and sanitizing equipment, but I would stick to PBW and Star San. It's better safe than sorry—this is not where you will have fun experimenting with homebrewing! PBW and Star San do not affect your equipment by corrosion over time and can be used on all equipment types.

Brewing Helpful Hints.

Let's talk about enzymes, the compounds that break down the grains during your mash. The two main enzymes at work during the mash are alpha and beta amylase.

Alpha amylase is the most active and the main enzyme. It results in more mouthfeel and a fuller-bodied beer. Beta amylase works with alpha amylase for a more complete fermentation.

A mash in the middle temperature range of 153° F Fahrenheit is desirable for getting both enzymes working. A lower mash temperature in the 150° F range emphasizes the beta amylase enzyme, which results in a more complete fermentation utilizing more of the simple sugars. This causes a thinner and drier beer with more alcohol. When using a lower mash temperature, then, it may be necessary to extend the mash to 90 minutes to give the alphas more time to work.

Speed Round

Here are a few last random tips:

I wouldn't mash out higher than 170° F, but the benefits of mashing out is usually only for very thick beers where you need to lower viscosity. This in turn makes the beer thinner and easier to lauter. In addition, mashing out and sparging at too high a temperature could lead to off flavors from tannins.

Long boils further the reduction of DMS (Dimethyl Sulfide), considered an off flavor in most beers. Pilsner Lagers are notorious for their DMS build up, but we can reduce DMS to where it's not perceptible to the taste.

Lower fermentation temperatures reduce fusel alcohol taste. Higher fermentation temperatures increase ester production. If fermentation temperature get too high, it can lead to high esters of solvent and/or alcohol flavors in the beer and this is generally frowned upon in most styles of beer.

Long aging periods are needed to clean up and level out high gravity beers.

For me, the most flavorful wort you could ever have is after one pass. That means no sparging or recirculation. If I do sparge and recirculate, it tends to be for a high gravity beer that I need more volume from and want to thin out a bit.

For water, at least use a percentage of filtered water, even if it's only 35 percent. Again, be sure to strip the chlorophenols, including chloramine. My general-purpose water dilution is 50/50.

For sour beers, I normally do a kettle sour by dumping in some pineapple skins, covering it with a cheese cloth, and leaving it exposed to the air for at least a day to inoculate with wild things like wild bacteria that creates lactic acid and wild yeast strains like Brett.

Souring is to taste; taste it each day until desired complexity and sourness. The pH value I normally like is between 3.3 and 4.3.

Sun Brewing Clone Recipes.

The majority of beers I've made are craft-brewed Borderland Avant-garde ales. My brewery was designed for this style of beer. This style is all about giving the people from our region something to enjoy and have a connection to.

Meados de Alien Ale, for instance, has apricots and New Mexican chile peppers in it. Apricots go extremely well with some chile peppers (malty sweet with a pinch of heat and slightly citrus sour!)—like in a chamoy sauce. The fruity citrus cuts through the heat of the pepper to achieve balance. Intercourse Ale was made with Abuelita Mexican chocolate—that is a very beloved ingredient in the borderlands.

I do make Das **Reinheitsgebot** beers and occasional lagers. In fact, if I had it my way, I would make lagers and ales equally. Hopefully, in my future expansion I can install more fermenters so I can create more lagers. I believe that lagers make some of the very best sour beers in the entire world. I've been experimenting with sour lagers recently and I like them more than sour ales.

I sincerely hope you enjoy my cookbook; I think there is something for everyone to enjoy. That's what I want more than anything: for people to enjoy making what they eat and drink.

True Craft Beer

The best craft beer comes from the homebrewers. Why? Brewing is really pragmatic; you have to always think about your bottom line. For example, everyone does the same basic processes, like sparging and recirculating, which are designed to extract more sugars from the mash. Breweries do this to save money… them pennies add up if you're distributing from coast to coast or even your own state. But that's different than saying it improves the flavor.

The most flavorful beer in the entire world comes from your renegade and skilled homebrewer because, if you are like me, you don't always adhere to all the standards and best practices. If I want the best possible wort, then I'll do one pass with no sparging or recirculation. I'm trying to make the best possible beer no matter the cost. That's the essence of craft beer.

(That said, I do sparge and recirculate when I want to lower the viscosity and ABV.)

Really, the key differentiator to me for craft beer is local, small-scale brewing that is not a commodity. Some people call these types of breweries boutique breweries; I call them real craft breweries, real punk rockers!

I love craft beer for a lot of the reasons other craft drinkers love it: for the culture, the flavors, the attitude—the fun! The community is very diverse which makes it powerful to connect to all beer lovers. In other words, it's about soul, not the almighty dollar.

If I had it my way, then there would be a huge explosion of even more craft breweries! I imagine a world where there is street beer on every corner and made out of a bucket.

This cookbook should be viewed as a guideline to boost you on your way to brewing good beer and cooking magnificent concoctions that are your own.

Note: All recipes are for 5.5 gallons.

Note: Boil times assume you are counting down. For example, if I say, "Boil for 60 minutes" and then "Add hops at the 45-minute mark," that means you will add hops when a countdown timer hits 45 mins, or 15 minutes into the boil.

My First Sun Beers.

Meados de Alien and Intercourse Ale are classic **Borderland Avant-garde** beers. They exemplify this style by infusing beloved ingredients from not only El Paso but the borderland region. Meados de Alien was inspired by an apricot chile jam I obtained from Hatch, New Mexico. I use apricots grown right here in Canutillo. Chiles are everywhere in El Paso. Intercourse Ale has the extremely loved Abuelita Mexican chocolate with cultural tri-city spices of star anise and cinnamon.

Meados de Alien Ale

11 lb. of American 2-row pale malt
2 lbs. of American crystal malt 60L
6 lbs. of apricots (pureed)
¼ lb. of red New Mexican chile peppers.

Note: If you don't have access to New Mexican chile peppers, then you could use any pepper you like. This is to taste; I use just a pinch for a very small undertone. Mild peppers you could use more of.

Mash at 155° F for 30 minutes.

Mash out at 165° F.

Note: Adding 2 gallons of water at 185° F will raise the temperature to approximately 165° F. If you're working with a 5.5 gallon batch, you'll need a mash tun at least 2 gallons larger. An 8- to 10-gallon mash tun would be ideal. I consider mashing out like this a form of sparging.

Sparge and Recirculate.

Boil for 60 minutes.

Add ½ oz. Nugget hops at the 45-minute mark.

Add 1 oz. of Ahtanum hops at the 5-minute mark.

Ferment with California Ale yeast or equivalent at 72° F.

Diacetyl Rest: Give diacetyl rest from the last few days of fermentation while not letting the temperature rise higher than 72° F.

Note: Mashing out at 165 decreases viscosity, but it's not hot enough to increase tannins (polyphenols).

OG 1.071
FG 1.018
ABV 6.9
IBU 26
SRM 14

There are three basic ways I've added the apricots to this beer. None is truly better than the other; it's more a question of style and taste.

1. **Secondary Fermentation** This is my preferred method because it achieves an amazing fruit aroma.
   Wash the apricots and add them to a stock pot full of water at 140° F and cook for 30 minutes. This ensures all bacteria will be killed. Anything over 102° F will start killing off any bacteria.
   Then add it to the secondary fermenter. This is the same concept as dry hopping.
2. **Primary Fermentation** The second option is to put the apricots from the stock pot into the primary fermenter. This isn't a bad option either and leads to a stronger apricot taste because it infuses longer. The aroma is still good, just not as strong as with Option 1.
3. **Boil** The third option is to puree the apricots and to add them in the last three minutes of the boil. The

longer the apricots boil in the beer, the more pectin will come out to haze your beer. I've never minded this at all, but when I first made Meados de Alien it was considered blasphemy in El Paso to have a little haze. Times have changed a lot since I've opened Sun Brewing and its trendy now.

Intercourse Ale

This was my first Mexican chocolate beer. Making a beer with Mexican chocolate has never been done before in El Paso and the borderlands. It was a revolutionary idea. Keep in mind nowadays it's pretty trendy but back only six years ago it was completely new to the region.

Making a Mexican chocolate beer is not as difficult to brew as with other chocolates because in general Mexican chocolate is made with ground roasted cocoa nibs, unrefined pure cane sugar, and spices like cinnamon. Mexican chocolate is one of the best chocolates in the world and I love to brew with it!

8 lbs. of American 2-row pale malt
1 lb. of American crystal malt 40L
1 lb. of American chocolate malt 350L
½ lb. of Abuelita Mexican chocolate
Mash at 157° F for 30 minutes.
Boil for 60 minutes.
Add ½ oz. Nugget hops at the 45-minute mark.
Add Abuelita Mexican chocolate at the 30-minute mark.
Ferment with California Ale yeast or equivalent at 70° F.
OG 1.049

FG 1.012
ABV 4.8
IBU 25
SRM 29

Sun IPA

This IPA didn't have a normal hop profile, so it was a bit of a risk for a town that was still learning about IPAs to begin with, but it turned out extremely well and people really loved it. There are no sacred cows in brewing IPAs anymore, so it fits right in these days.

This IPA has an earthy, spicy, floral, and citrus flavor. Sun IPA has a distinct grapefruit and floral aroma.

11 lbs. of American 2-row pale malt
1 lb. of American crystal malt 15L
½ tsp. of Irish moss
Mash at 153° F for 60 minutes.
No mash out.
Boil for 60 minutes.
Add 1 oz. Nugget hops at the 45-minute mark.
Add 1 oz. Tettnanger hops at the 30-minute mark.
Add 1 oz. Ahtanum hops at the 15-minute mark.
Add ½ tsp. of Irish moss at the 15-minute mark.
Add 1 oz. Ahtanum hops at the 10-minute mark.
Add 1 oz. Ahtanum hops at the 5-minute mark.
Dry hop the last five days of fermentation with 3 oz. of Ahtanum.
Ferment with California Ale yeast or equivalent at 72° F.

OG 1.062
FG 1.015
ABV 6
IBU 60
SRM 5

Tamale Top Ale

This was one of the first beers I released at Sun Brewing, and it was first showcased at Tosca Stone Oven Pizzeria for a special keg tapping—it gave them a record night. I'm also proud to say this was the first El Paso craft beer ever distributed.

This beer was considered outrageous at the time—a beer made with sweet tamales? Nowadays in El Paso, however, dessert beers or bread beers are not so taboo, especially since the big craft beer giants made dessert beers a national trend.

Sweet tamales are made with masa (which is a type of cornmeal), raisins, and spices such as cinnamon and star anise. Some people add brown or other sugars to sweeten them up a bit.

The tamales serve as a fermentable you can throw right

in the mash alongside the normal grain bill. This adds more simple sugars to the beer, drying it out while giving it a slight tart taste with hints of spice. It varies depending on the type of sweet tamale, of course. For example, I've made a sweet tamale with pineapples and pecan nuts. I use a different sweet tamale every year.

I've made Tamale Top Ale using dried sweet tamales for anywhere between 30 and 50 percent of the grain bill.

This recipe was the original recipe for Tamale Top Ale but you could also add small amounts of star anise and cinnamon if you wanted a more pronounced spicy flavor. The original flavor had a very slight tart character from raisins, along with very slight hints of spice. The crystal malt 40L gave the beer caramel notes.

10 lbs. of American 2-row pale malt

2.5 lbs. of American crystal malt 40L

5 lbs. of dried sweet tamales (See Pub Beer Food in Part Four) **add the dried sweet tamales with the rest of your grain bill for starch conversion.*

½ tsp. of Irish moss

Mash at 155° F for 60 minutes.

No mash out. Sparge and Recirculate.

Boil for 60 minutes.

Add ½ oz. Nugget hops at the 45-minute mark.

Add ½ oz. Ahtanum hops at the 15-minute mark.

Add ½ tsp. of Irish moss at the 15-minute mark.

Ferment with California Ale yeast or equivalent at 72° F.

OG 1.062

FG 1.016

ABV 6.1
IBU 23
SRM 12

Classic Ales.

American pale ales are an all-around go-to beer for just about anything. They are good for making bread because they do not impart too much bitterness from the baking process and give an accentuated fruity taste. They easily go with other foods like my Beer Can Chicken.

Left Turn at Albuquerque Pale Ale

The goal of this American pale ale was to have a good bitterness but that is not as strong as an IPA, coupled with an aroma that is comparable to an IPA. This is so that you can enjoy the amazing hop flavor and aroma without the strong bitterness of a traditional IPA.

11 lbs. of American 2-row pale malt
1 lb. of Vienna malt
⅓ lb. of crystal malt 75L
Mash at 155° F for 60 minutes.
Boil for 60 minutes.
Add ½ oz. Simcoe hops at the 45-minute mark.
Add ½ oz. Citra hops at the 15-minute mark.
Add ½ oz. Citra hops at the 5-minute mark.
Ferment with California Ale yeast or equivalent at 72° F.
Dry hop the last five days of fermentation with 1 oz. of Mosaic.

OG 1.062
FG 1.015
ABV 6
IBU 35
SRM 6.25

I love to pair Belgian pale ales with my fried chicken! You could also use ale for beer batter for some fish and chips. It's also a versatile beer to cook with. I use it in breads and ice cream. It's great for seafood pasta. Boil the pasta in a pot filled with ale and serve with some beer cheese crawfish or beer shrimp scampi.

Atreyu Belgian Pale Ale

8 lbs. of Pilsner malt
1 lb. of Carapils malt
½ lb. of Victory malt
Mash at 153° F for 60 minutes.

Sparge and Recirculate.
Boil for 60 minutes.
Add ½ oz. Nugget hops at the 45-minute mark.
Add ½ oz. Ahtanum hops at the 5-minute mark.
Ferment with Belgian Schelde Ale yeast or equivalent at 67° F.

OG 1.050
FG 1.010
ABV 5.3
IBU 25
SRM 6

<u>Belgian amber ales</u> are excellent for baking bread. I love using them for my beer-battered frog legs.

Falkor Belgian Amber Ale

This is another versatile beer that I use to cook with for just about anything because it's not too hoppy or bitter and has a nice malty flavor accentuated by the flavors from yeast strain. This would also be great for some beer cheese.

8 lbs. of Pilsner malt
1 lb. of Carapils malt
½ lb. of Victory malt
1.2 lbs. of Belgian amber candi syrup
Mash at 153° F for 60 minutes.
Sparge and Recirculate.
Boil for 60 minutes.
Add ½ oz. Nugget hops at the 45-minute mark.
Add ½ oz. Ahtanum hops at the 5-minute mark.

Ferment with Belgian Ardennes Ale yeast or equivalent at 66° F.

OG 1.058
FG 1.012
ABV 6
IBU 25
SRM 12

IPAs are the trickiest of styles to cook with but can also be very rewarding. There used to really be only one style of IPA, the West Coast IPA, and that is still my go-to style. There are all kinds of IPAs, nowadays. I personally like to pair the fruity, less bitter IPAs with my barbecue straight off the grill, like some spicy BBQ ribs. For cooking, I'll throw fruity IPAs in a vinaigrette or a marinade for some skirt steaks or to make an NEIPA Beer Chicken.

Now, for the granddaddy of IPAs: the West Coast IPA. I love that bitter bite. Most people around the borderlands pair IPAs with Mexican food; it's a natural fit because the IPA balances out the spices. But for cooking, I use it a lot with soups, especially with a little spice and cheese. West Coast IPAs are great for marinades and for steaming foods. I'll make some IPA beer-steamed sausages, steamed potatoes, or steamed flautas. I also cook and pair them with my grilled octopus, then dump the baby octopi in my seafood **discada**. Cooking with IPA is the most fascinating, underexplored area of cooking with beer.

DAVID SLOCUM

Nincompoop Continuously Hopped IPA

Knocked out in the 3rd of the National IPA Championship.

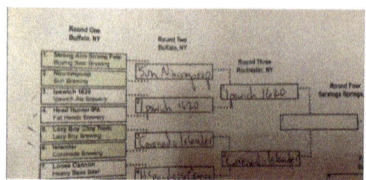

This was a crazy beer that I dreamed up, brewed with hop water (which, of course, I also made). I named this beer Nincompoop because I felt like a big dummy manually throwing in the hops continuously in hopes of achieving a superior-tasting IPA. The work was well worth it, because I did in fact create a world-class beer. I was so happy just to be able to advance in the National IPA Championships. I was beat by Ipswitch, who made it deep into the competition and almost won it all. This really showed how Sun Brewing was making continuous progress in my goals of making some of the very best beer in the world.

11 lbs. of American 2-row pale malt

0.7 lb. of American crystal malt 15L
½ lb. of acid malt
½ tsp. of Irish moss

Mash at 153° F for 60 minutes with hop water.

Note: You'll want to heat the water to approximately 165° F, first, and then mix in the grains. Let it drop to 153° F and hold it there.

Hop Water.

2 oz. of whole-cone Ahtanum hops per gallon of water. See IPA water profile under the water section to prepare IPA water profile for hop water. You will need something to steep the hops in like a tea ball, tea bag, or hop sock (this also helps with removing them afterward). There is a lot of room for experimentation with hop water. You could cold press or you could heat up the water. You could also add sugar and other adjuncts. When I made Nincompoop, I steeped the hops for 15 minutes while heating the water to reach my target temperature for the mash.

Note: When making hop water, you'll want to pick a hop that is low in alpha acids to avoid a harsh flavor. You'll want to choose a hop that is for aroma primarily.

Boil for 60 minutes. (Here comes the fun part.)
Add 0.3 oz. Nugget hops at the 60-minute mark.
Add 0.3 oz. Nugget hops at the 55-minute mark.
Add 0.2 oz. Simcoe hops at the 50-minute mark.
Add 0.2 oz. Simcoe hops at the 45-minute mark.
Add 0.2 oz. Chinook hops at the 40-minute mark.

Add 0.2 oz. Chinook hops at the 35-minute mark.
Add 0.2 oz. Ahtanum hops at the 30-minute mark.
Add 0.2 oz. Ahtanum hops at the 25-minute mark.
Add 0.2 oz. Ahtanum hops at the 20-minute mark.
Add 0.2 oz. Ahtanum hops and ½ tsp. of Irish moss at the 15-minute mark.
Add 0.2 oz. Citra hops at the 10-minute mark.
Add 0.2 oz. Citra hops at the 5-minute mark.
Add 0.2 oz. Citra hops at the 0-minute mark.
Dry hop the last 10 days of fermentation with 3 oz. of Ahtanum.

Ferment with California Ale yeast or equivalent at 72° F.
OG 1.060
FG 1.015
ABV 6
IBU 80
SRM 5

Gypsy Dude IPA.

People loved this beer and I named a lot of beers using the word "gypsy" because I myself always felt like a gypsy. My entire life was basically traveling and being an outsider in someone else's culture. Gypsy fit me.

10 lbs. of American 2-row pale malt
½ lb. of American crystal malt 10L
½ lb. of corn syrup
½ tsp. of Irish moss
Mash at 153° F for 60 minutes.

Boil for 60 minutes.
Add ½ oz. Nugget hops at the 45-minute mark.
Add ½ oz. Chinook hops at the 30-minute mark.
Add 1 oz. Cascade hops at the 15-minute mark.
Add ½ tsp. of Irish moss at the 15-minute mark.
Add 1 oz. Centennial hops at the 5-minute mark.
Ferment with California Ale yeast or equivalent at 72° F.

Dry hop the last five days of fermentation with 1 oz. of Cascade and 1 oz. of Centennial.

OG 1.056
FG 1.010
ABV 6
IBU 60
SRM 4

You Don't Know Jack! Fruit IPA

This is essentially a jackfruit black IPA. It has an unexpected flavor that you'll either savor or spit out. The fusion of flavors in this beer reminds me of a sweet pulled pork sandwich. Believe me, it works!

10 lbs. of American 2-row pale malt
½ lb. of crystal malt 10L
½ lb. of crystal malt 80L
½ lb. of chocolate malt
½ lb. of Midnight Wheat
½ tsp. of Irish moss
Mash at 153° F for 60 minutes.
Sparge and Recirculate.

Boil for 60 minutes.

Add ½ oz. Nugget hops at the 45-minute mark.

Add ½ oz. Simcoe hops at the 30-minute mark.

Add 1 oz. Cascade hops and ½ tsp. of Irish moss at the 15-minute mark.

Add 1 oz. Mosaic hops at the 5-minute mark.

Add 8 lbs. of jackfruit at the 5-minute mark.

Ferment with California Ale yeast or equivalent at 72° F.

Dry hop the last five days of fermentation with 2 oz. of Mosaic.

Note: To prepare the jackfruit, you'll want to core it and take off the skin.

OG 1.059

FG 1.015

ABV 5.8

IBU 57

SRM 34

This *malt liquor* is dry, neutral-tasting, and low in bitterness. This pairs well with just about anything because of its neutral flavor. I personally use it to cook with just about everything from shellfish to beer discada. It's great to boil food in or parboil meat, like a big pork shoulder. I'll use this beer to sip on with a grilled Tomahawk steak or even a crawfish boil. It's more to complement food rather than adding a lot of flavor. Being neutral in flavor doesn't make a beer bad, it's just a different flavor profile. I personally love a neutral-tasting beer with a clean, crisp taste and a slight fusel alcohol warmness as I drink.

Malt liquors get a bad rap nowadays. It's more of a

branding thing than anything else. If you look at the history of malt liquor, it was once a high society beer served at country clubs. Mass production, usually in 40 oz. bottles, coupled with being sold cheaper and made cheaper, had huge consequences. It took a major reputation hit and people began to change the way they looked at malt liquor.

Any beer style can be cheapened. Truthfully, there is no difference in a malt liquor than, say, a honey pale ale that's at least 5 percent ABV. It's all branding, really. You tell somebody, "Hey, I've got this great honey pale ale made with local wildflower honey," and people will be very enticed.

Canutillo Malt Liquor

Made with chicales and blue agave.
11 lbs. of American 2-row pale malt
1.4 lb. of crystal malt 10L
1 lb. of Carapils malt
4 lb. of chicales
0.4 lb. of Blue Agave
Note: If you don't have access to chicales then you could use raw corn shucked.

Cereal Mash.

This is a separate mash from the all-grain mash. You can do this in stock pot on the stove.

1. Rinse and clean the chicales

2. Fill a 5-gallon pot with 3 gallons of purified water
3. Put the chicales in the pot
4. Heat pot on low to medium heat
5. Stir the chicales every few minutes or so.
6. Once temperature reaches 155° F, hold it there for 15 minutes.
7. Then, turn the heat up until the water boils.
8. Boil for 30 minutes while stirring frequently

All-Grain Mash.

Mash at 155° F for 60 minutes.
Sparge and Recirculate.
Mash out at 165° F.
Boil for 90 minutes.
Dump chicales in sometime in the first 15 minutes of the boil.
Add 0.3 oz. Nugget hops at the 45-minute mark.
Add 0.4 lb. of blue agave at the 0- minute mark.
Ferment with California Ale yeast or equivalent at 64° F.
Diacetyl Rest: Give a diacetyl rest from the last few days of fermentation while not letting the temperature rise higher than 70° F.
OG 1.070
FG 1.017
ABV 6.9
IBU 12
SRM 5
<u>Amber and Red Ales</u> are great for barbecue! I'll pair Irish

reds with some Texas brisket or an amber ale with spicy BBQ ribs or my Chamoy Wings. They are great for palate cleansing. I use amber and red ales a lot for making bread; I think it's the best for bread making. It's also great for amber ale paella or for boiling rice. Irish Red Lamb Stew is decadent. These are great beers to cook with and for food pairing.

Ard Draoi Irish Red

I honestly don't know how to pronounce Ard Draoi because it's Gaelic. Something like *ahrd dree*, but you have to kind of stop the first "d" with your tongue and trill the second one. I worked with the Irish on a daily basis as an automation engineer and my Irish friends from Donegal, Ireland, helped me name this beer (but not to say it). In the Gaelic language, *ard draoi* means high priest and would translate to English as archdruid. This beer is one of three in my Project Clover series along with Cheeky Devil Tropical Stout and Angels' Share Foreign Extra Stout.

9 lbs. of American 2-row pale malt
0.4 lb. of crystal malt 40L
0.4 lb. of crystal malt 120L
0.4 lb. of roasted barley malt
Mash at 155° F for 60 minutes.
Sparge and Recirculate.
Boil for 90 minutes.
Add ½ oz. Nugget hops at the 45-minute mark.
Ferment with Irish Ale yeast or equivalent at 66° F.
OG 1.051

FG 1.013
ABV 5
IBU 25
SRM 18

Holy Huerache Amber Ale

Made with Canutillo lemons.

This is a basic amber ale with a hint of lemon. A malty, slightly sweet ale with a touch of sour from a local Canutillo lemon tree.

8 lbs. of American 2-row pale malt
1 lb. of crystal malt 80L
1 lb. of Victory malt
2 oz. of lemon zest
2 oz. of lemon juice
Mash at 155° F for 60 minutes.
Boil for 60 minutes.
Add ½ oz. Nugget hops at the 45-minute mark.
Add 2 oz. of lemon zest at the 5-minute mark.
Add 2 oz. of freshly squeezed lemon juice at the 3-minute mark.
Add ½ oz. Citra hops at the 10-minute mark.
Ferment with California Ale yeast or equivalent at 69° F.
OG 1.055
FG 1.014
ABV 5.4
IBU 32

SRM 13

Old School Love Altbier

This beer has bitterness but not like a bitter beer. The bitterness is balanced with the malt character. The yeast gives it a nice pinch of a German yeast character for a flavorful, well-balanced beer.

8 lbs. of Pilsner malt
1 lb. of Munich malt
4 oz. of CaraMunich malt
Mash at 150° F for 90 minutes.
Note: The longer mash ensures beta amylase conversion, which results in a more attenuated, drier, and thinner beer.
Boil for 60 minutes.
Add ½ oz. Nugget hops at the 60-minute mark.
Add ½ oz. Tettnanger hops at the 15-minute mark.
Ferment with German Ale yeast or equivalent at 69° F.
OG 1.048
FG 1.012
ABV 4.7
IBU 28
SRM 18

Ice beer is great for frying foods. The higher the ABV from freeze concentration, the better the batter. Any beer can be ice brewed, but I tend to ice dark beers. Amber ice ales are great for pairing with my fermented beer-battered foods, especially my fermented beer-battered fried chicken. It's also great for making the beer batter, of course! The malty richness and alcohol content make for a nice crispy and flavorful crust.

Ice beers have a warmness to them in the finish, which I personally really love in any beer.

It seems like this style is becoming extinct among craft brewers, which makes me sad. It will be up to the homebrewers to keep it alive!

Keep in mind that freeze-concentrating a beer does more than add alcohol, it also amplifies the flavor of the beer by concentrating it. Keep this in mind when designing your recipe.

The Working Man Ice Ale

9.5 lbs. of Pilsner malt
1 lb. of Victory malt
½ lb. of crystal malt 40L
½ lb. of crystal malt 120L
Mash at 155° F for 60 minutes.
Sparge and Recirculate.
Boil for 90 minutes.

Add ⅓ oz. Nugget hops at the 45-minute mark.

Ferment at 62° F with California Ale yeast or equivalent.

Diacetyl Rest: Give a diacetyl rest from the last few days of fermentation while not letting the temperature rise higher than 70° F.

When it comes to fractional distillation, also known as freeze distillation, you are freezing your finished beer to reduce it by a percentage, therefore concentrating the alcohol and taste in the beer.

If you have a 5-gallon batch of beer that is 5.6 percent ABV and you freeze the entire 5 gallons and reduce it by half, then you would have doubled the concentration, meaning you would have taken the beer from 5.6 percent ABV to 11.2 percent ABV. I don't freeze entire batches. A 10–20 percent concentration is good enough. This not only concentrates the beer, it amplifies the taste. Keep this in mind when you are choosing your grains to brew with.

In this case, I reduce 20 percent of the batch by half, which raises the ABV by 1.1 points. Consequently, I went from a 5.6 percent beer to a 6.7 percent beer.

Ice Procedure.

1. Take two cleaned and sanitized one-gallon jugs and fill them each with a half-gallon of finished beer. That's half a gallon per jug for a total of one full gallon.
2. Put the beer jugs in the freezer.
   Note: I used the purified water jugs that I used to brew the beer for this.

3. When the water turns to ice, pull the jugs out and drain the residual liquid into the bottling bucket.

    Note: The residual alcohol will drain out because of the different freezing temperatures of alcohol and water. This will take several hours to do. You'll see the ice inside the jugs and the concentrated beer dripping out. Once you've reduced the beer by half, then you're done. Reduced by half means you've drained out half the volume of what you started at. For example, if you froze 6 gallons, then when you've drained the residual alcohol to 3 gallons, you've hit your mark.

4. You're ready to bottle!

OG 1.057

FG 1.014

ABV 5.6 + 1.1 ABV point after freeze concentration to equal 6.7 ABV

IBU 15

SRM 12

Brown ales go excellent with my roasted goat tacos. This beer is great for marinating meats, roasting meats, and making bread. A brown ale beef stew or a brown ale roasted duck would be an excellent choice.

Wocka Wocka Brown Ale

This is also the base to my You Don't Know Jack! Fruit Brown IPA. If you wanted to get a little wild, then add 1 lb. of

Jack Fruit to the last three minutes of the boil plus a lot more Cascade hops to send it into the IPA hop range.

8 lbs. of Maris Otter malt
1 lb. of crystal malt 80L
½ lb. of Victory malt
½ lb. of chocolate malt
Mash at 153° F for 60 minutes.
Boil for 60 minutes.
Add ½ oz. Nugget hops at the 45-minute mark.
Add ⅓ oz. Cascade hops at the 10-minute mark.
Ferment with California Ale yeast or equivalent at 69° F.
OG 1.050
FG 1.013
ABV 5
IBU 25
SRM 23

Woo-Woo Brown Porter

A brown porter is softer and more caramel flavor than a porter but roastier than a brown ale.

8 lbs. of American 2-row pale malt
1 lb. of crystal malt 40L
1 lb. of Brown malt
½ lb. of chocolate malt
Mash at 153° F for 60 minutes.
Boil for 60 minutes.
Add ½ oz. Nugget hops at the 45-minute mark.

Add ⅓ oz. Ahtanum hops at the 10-minute mark.
Ferment with California Ale yeast or equivalent at 69° F.
OG 1.051
FG 1.013
ABV 5.1
IBU 25
SRM 23

I find myself cooking with <u>stout</u> beer probably more than any other beer. It's great for making decadent desserts like my stout beer brownies or for making stout lamb pie. It's also great for sauces, glazes, or for making my Stout Beer-Nog around Christmas season.

Cheeky Devil Tropical Stout

This beer was one of three beers inspired by my travels to Ireland and part of my Project Clover series of beers, including Ard Draoi Irish Red and Angels' Share Foreign Extra Stout.

The West Indies porter was the forerunner to foreign extra stout and tropical stout is like its first cousin. These beers were intended for export to Africa and the Caribbean in the 1800's.

This beer is similar to the FES but with more sweetness and fruitiness. It is also often fermented with lager yeast strains, as in the recipe below. Tropical stouts use indigenous grains and adjuncts, which is what I always shoot for if I can pull it off with my beers. If you have access to local ingredients that aren't precisely what I use, man, go for it!

Tropical stouts are smoother and less bitter than traditional stouts, and I personally love drinking them on the beach. It's a major misconception that only certain types of beers (like American lagers or light lagers) are good beach beers. Stouts can be very refreshing to drink while hanging out on the beach or in hot climates like the desert or tropical environments.

As you can see from the picture below, I like a lot of head to my beer. It's a personal preference.

9 lbs. of English 2-row pale malt
½ lb. of Victory malt
½ lb. of roasted barley malt
½ lb. of crystal malt 40L
½ lb. of crystal malt 120L
½ lb. of chocolate malt
Mash at 155° F for 60 minutes.
Sparge and Recirculate.
Boil for 90 minutes.
Add 1 oz. Nugget hops at the 45-minute mark.
Ferment with American Ale yeast and San Francisco Lager Yeast at 60° F.
Diacetyl Rest: Give a diacetyl rest from the last few days

of fermentation while not letting the temperature rise higher than 72° F.

OG 1.056
FG 1.014
ABV 5.6
IBU 24
SRM 36

Angels' Share Foreign Extra Stout

This beer is one of three in my Project Clover series along with Cheeky Devil Tropical Stout and Ard Draoi Irish Red.

Angels' Share is a bold, full-bodied beer with hints of sweetness. It's a bigger-flavored beer which has a warming alcohol content. This beer is similar to Tropical Stout but with less sweetness and fruitiness.

The artwork from the picture below was done from my daughter Natalie for this beer. She is in high school and wants to work for Disney doing animation.

11 lbs. of English 2-row pale malt

1 lb. of roasted barley malt
1 lb. of crystal malt 80L
1 lb. of chocolate malt
Mash at 157° F for 60 minutes.
Sparge and Recirculate.
Boil for 60 minutes.
Add 1 oz. Nugget hops at the 45-minute mark.
Ferment with California Ale yeast or equivalent at 67° F.
Diacetyl Rest: Give a diacetyl rest from the last few days of fermentation while not letting the temperature rise higher than 72° F.

OG 1.070
FG 1.017
ABV 6.9
IBU 30
SRM 44

Sun Arkhangelisk Russian Imperial Stout

This beer is the biggest and the boldest of all the stouts. The trick to this beer is to not make it too solvently with too much fusel alcohol burn. We can avoid this by a lower fermentation temperature coupled with a long aging period to clean up and level out the beer. I don't know how many times I've made a big bold beer and thought it was substandard all to find out after aging it for several months that it's become a good beer. We also need to ensure this beer is highly attenuated to avoid cloying.

When I created this recipe, I added the C10 in order to add a touch of sweetness to the dark coffee and roasted flavors. It's more of a personal preference.

14 lbs. of American 2-row pale malt
1.4 lb. of roasted barley malt
1.4 lb. of crystal malt 10L
1.4 lb. of crystal malt 120L
1.4 lb. of chocolate malt
Mash at 157° F for 60 minutes.
Mash out at 165° F F.
Sparge and Recirculate.
Boil for 60 minutes.

Add 1 oz. Nugget hops at the 45-minute mark.

Ferment with California Ale yeast or equivalent at 67° F.

Diacetyl Rest: Give a diacetyl rest from the last few days of fermentation while not letting the temperature rise higher than 72° F.

OG 1.097
FG 1.024
ABV 9.6
IBU 33
SRM 50

Classic Lagers.

Black ice beers are great for beer batter because of the richness of the beer infused in the batter and the crispiness the higher alcohol gives to the finished product. Ice beers are along the same lines as malt liquors in the sense that they have a warmness in the finish. Ice beers need to make a comeback in the craft community in a major way because it seems like not too many people are making them.

Black ice beers, in particular, are not your standard beers.

Sun Black Ice Lager

This particular black ice lager is just the right amount of malty and chocolatey, which makes it a versatile beer to cook with. I'll use it a lot for beer batter. I'll make some beer-battered chicken wings with this one. I like it for my beer burgers or beer crinkle fries. It's also great as a meat tenderizer.

Here's my recipe for my clean and refreshing black ice.

3.1 lbs. of Pilsner malt
4 lbs. of Munich malt
3 lbs. of Vienna malt
⅓ lb. of chocolate malt
⅓ lb. of Midnight Wheat
Mash at 155° F for 60 minutes.
Sparge and Recirculate.
Boil for 90 minutes.
Add ⅓ oz. Nugget hops at the 45-minute mark.
Ferment at 55° F with Old Bavarian yeast or other appropriate yeast for at least a month. Then transfer to secondary for at least another month of lagering.

Note: As with all my beers, even my lagers, this is bottle conditioned.

Diacetyl Rest: Give a diacetyl rest to 65° F for at least three days.

Freeze distillation, also known as freeze concentration, basically means that you are freezing water out of your finished beer to reduce it by a percentage, therefore concentrating the alcohol.

If you have a 5-gallon batch of beer that is 5 percent ABV and you freeze the entire 5 gallons and reduce it by half, then you would have doubled the concentration, meaning you would have taken the beer from 5 percent ABV to 10 percent. I don't freeze entire batches. A 10–20 percent concentration is good enough. This not only concentrates the beer, it amplifies the taste.

In this case, I reduce 20 percent by half, which raises the ABV by 1 point. Consequently, I went from a 5 percent beer to a 6 percent beer.

Refer to Working Man Ice Ale for ice procedure.

OG 1.051

FG 1.013

ABV 5 plus one ABV point after freeze concentration to equal 6 abv.

IBU 15

SRM 34

Vienna lagers are great for cooking because of their dry and crisp finish with hints of caramel and toasty, bready notes. I've made some pork stew with this one and some Vienna lager pies. I've also cooked Vienna lager chicken tacos in a cast iron pan. I'll use it for a Vienna lager beer bread pizza or for

Vienna lager **molotes** stuffed with cheese or spiced meats. It's a great beer to cook with. It pairs well with a lot of different foods, but I use it a lot for pairing with my Beer Brats and for boiling my beer brats.

The Third Edge Vienna Lager.

This is my version of a Vienna lager. I wanted only Pilsner and Vienna malt with no adjuncts. This beer is truly magnificent, full of subtleties. The yeast character really steals the show and gives it a pleasant mouthfeel.

I named this beer The Third Edge in honor of my old friend that I went to Coronado High School with who is also a local KLAQ DJ and has been a musician for decades. Raymon Arreola does it for love and passion. I have always respected that, and I named this beer after his original band. Ray and his original bandmate Sam Dayoub still perform together to this day.

6 lbs. of Pilsner malt
5 lbs. of Vienna malt

Mash at 153° F for 60 minutes.

Boil for 90 minutes.

Add ⅓ oz. Nugget hops at the 45-minute mark.

Ferment at 55° F with Old Bavarian yeast or other appropriate yeast for at least a month. Then transfer to a secondary fermenter for at least another month of lagering.

Note: As with all my beers, even my lagers, this is bottle conditioned.

Diacetyl Rest: When you are almost done fermenting, within a notch or two of your final gravity, give a diacetyl rest at 65° F for at least three days but no longer than seven days. Diacetyl rest is a lager procedure where you raise the temperature approximately 10 degrees to clean up diacetyl in the beer. Diacetyl gives a butter flavor to the beer and is a technical flaw in some beer styles. However, a little diacetyl is considered acceptable in some styles like a Czech pilsner or a Scottish ale.

OG 1.055
FG 1.014
ABV 5.4
IBU 15

SRM 5

<u>American lager</u>

Sun American Lager

8 lbs. of American 2-row pale malt
1 lb. of flaked corn
1 lb. of acid malt
1 lb. of Carapils malt
Mash at 153° F for 90 minutes to ensure complete conversion.
Sparge and Recirculate.
Boil for 90 minutes to reduce DMS.

Add ⅓ oz. Nugget hops at the 45-minute mark.

Add ⅓ oz. Saaz hops at the 15-minute mark.

Ferment at 50° F with American Lager yeast for at least a month. Then transfer to a secondary fermenter for at least another month. Finally, lager for another month or until desired clarity and finish.

Note: As with all my beers, even my lagers, this is bottle conditioned.

Diacetyl Rest: Give a diacetyl rest to 65° F for three days.

OG 1.054
FG 1.010
ABV 5.8
IBU 29
SRM 4

O'Slocum's Red Malt Beverage

This is a spinoff of O'Doul's malt beverage, but I wanted to make it a malty ale to increase mouthfeel. There are a lot of older guys who used to drink and still want to drink but can't for health reasons. With O'Slocum's, they can still drink a malt beverage that tastes like a beer.

5 lbs. of American 2-row pale malt

⅓ lb. of crystal malt 40L

⅓ lb. of crystal malt 120L

⅓ lb. of roasted barley malt

Mash at 160° F for 60 minutes.

Note: We are raising the mash temperature to have more dextrins and more unfermentable sugars because we want more mouthfeel for the low grain bill and the alcohol being boiled out. We still want this beverage to taste like a beer.

Boil for 60 minutes.

Add ½ oz. Nugget hops at the 45-minute mark.

Ferment with Irish Ale yeast or equivalent at 72° F.

OG 1.029
FG 1.010
ABV 2.5
IBU 30
SRM 14

Boiling Out Alcohol.

After the beer is done fermenting, add 1 gallon of water and boil it again for 30 minutes. This will evaporate all alcohol at least to 0.05 percent and add back some of the water lost to the boil.

Seasonals.

Valentine's Day

The People of the Sun Jamaica Ale

Hibiscus is magnificent—everything from its tart, herbal berry-like undertones to its extravagant appearance. It colors the beer a beautiful, velvety, crimson color.

This makes a perfect Valentine's Day beer to savor with a banana split all the way until springtime approaches.

10 lbs. of American 2-row pale malt

1 lb. of American crystal malt 15L

½ lb. of hibiscus (I normally buy these flowers at a local Mexican grocery store, like Victor's Rio Grande Supermarket in Canutillo. In a Mexican supermarket they are referred to as Jamaica.)

½ tsp. of Irish moss
Mash at 155° F for 60 minutes.
Sparge and Recirculate.
Boil for 60 minutes.
Add ⅓ oz. Nugget hops at the 45-minute mark.
Add hibiscus flowers at the 20-minute mark.
Add ½ tsp. of Irish moss at the 15-minute mark.
Ferment with California Ale yeast or equivalent at 66° F.
OG 1.055
FG 1.014
ABV 5.4
IBU 15
SRM 5

Halloween

Cinderella Loves Ale

This was my first Pumpkin beer and I try to make it every year to release in late October to catch the holiday season.

You can make this a dark pumpkin ale if you add a darker crystal malt and chocolate malt. You could even char and smoke the pumpkin.

10 lbs. of American 2-row pale malt
½ lb. of American crystal malt 15L
½ lb. of amber malt
10 lb. Cinderella Pumpkin (see below)
½ tsp. of Irish moss
Pumpkin spice mix (see below)

Mash at 155° F for 60 minutes.
Sparge and Recirculate.

Cinderella Pumpkin.

There are numerous ways to prepare the Cinderella pumpkin. You can grill it to get a charred, smokey flavor, or you can bake it until tender. You could also puree it. What I do is slice the pumpkin fresh with no pre-cooking. I use nice big slices, sometimes only quartering it. Then I lightly sprinkle the pumpkin spice mix over the slices.

Cinderella pumpkins have the greatest taste of all the pumpkins in my view and impart a great pumpkin taste in the beer.

Pumpkin Spice Mix.

- 1 tsp. cinnamon
- 1 tsp. ginger
- 1 tsp. cloves
- 1 tsp. nutmeg

Boil for 60 minutes.
Add ⅓ oz. Nugget hops at the 45-minute mark.
Add sliced Cinderella pumpkin at the 30-minute mark.
Add ½ tsp. of Irish moss at the 15-minute mark.
Ferment with California Ale yeast or equivalent at 72° F.
OG 1.057
FG 1.014
ABV 5.6

IBU 14
SRM 6

Canutillo Hoppy Vampires' Brew.

This beer is my Halloween beer. I release it almost every year.

9 lbs. of American 2-row pale malt
1 lb. of American crystal malt 15L
½ lb. of CaraRed malt
Pinch of hibiscus
½ tsp. of Irish moss
Mash at 155° F for 60 minutes.
Boil for 60 minutes.
Add ⅓ oz. Nugget hops at the 45-minute mark.
Add hibiscus flowers at the 20-minute mark.
Add ½ tsp. of Irish moss at the 15-minute mark.
Add 2 oz. of Cascade hops at the 15-minute mark.

Ferment with California Ale yeast or equivalent at 66° F.
OG 1.053
FG 1.013
ABV 5.2
IBU 36
SRM 5

Frankenstein Hybrid Ale

This was my first hybrid ale. By "hybrid" I mean half wine and half beer. It's still one of the best tasting hybrid beers I've ever made. It would be almost impossible to duplicate because of the dependency on a local vineyard to produce the exact same Syrah grape blend. I've never been able to get the exact same blend, consequently I name it something related, like "The Monster's Bride Hybrid Ale."

This Syrah grape blend was straight from a local vineyard called Mesa Vista. It was a sweet red blend of Syrah grapes. Use whatever you can get your hands on.

I named it Frankenstein for a few reasons, one of which was because this beer is a hybrid beer of wine grapes with wine yeast with ale. Also, when I received the grapes after harvest, it was around Halloween, so the name seemed perfect!

10 lbs. of American 2-row pale malt
1 lb. of American crystal malt 40L
1 lb. of American crystal malt 120L
1 lb. of Victory malt
2 lbs. of Syrah grape blend
½ tsp. of Irish moss

(If you don't have access to Syrah grapes, then you could use any comparable grape blend. If you don't have access to anything, then you could use grape juice from your local grocery store.) You would still need to use wine yeast and ale yeast.

Mash at 153° F for 60 minutes.

Sparge and Recirculate.

Boil for 60 minutes.

Add ½ oz. Nugget hops at the 45-minute mark.

Add ½ oz. Cascade hops at the 10-minute mark.

Add ½ tsp. of Irish moss at the 15-minute mark.

Ferment with California Ale yeast and Red Wine Yeast at 66° F.

Add Syrah grape blend, to a stock pot full of water at 140° F. Cook for 30 minutes. This ensures all bacteria will be killed. Anything over 102° F will start killing off any bacteria.

Then add it to the secondary fermenter. This is the same concept as dry hopping, except the yeast will ferment the must to give additional flavor. The flavor will become more pronounced like dry hopping because we are dumping it in the fermentation to infuse.

OG 1.067

FG 1.016

ABV 6.7

IBU 25

SRM 18

Christmas

Sun Calientito Ale

This beer is a Christmas Holiday season beer inspired by my wife's family's traditional Christmas holiday **calientito**.

10 lbs. of American 2-row pale malt
1 lb. of American crystal malt 40L
1 lb. of Victory malt
½ gallon of calientito (see Beverages in Part Four)
½ tsp. of Irish moss
Mash at 157° F for 60.
Sparge and Recirculate.
Boil for 60 minutes.
Add ½ oz. Nugget hops at the 45-minute mark.
Add ½ oz. Citra hops at the 10-minute mark.
Add ½ tsp. of Irish moss at the 15-minute mark.
Ferment with California Ale yeast or equivalent at 72° F.
OG 1.062
FG 1.015
ABV 6.1
IBU 30
SRM 9

Gingerbread Man Ale

This beer is made with spontaneous-beer gingerbread and is one of my Christmas-holiday brews. You can use classic gingerbread as a substitute.

6 lbs. of American 2-row pale malt
1 lb. of American crystal malt 40L
1 lb. of Victory malt
4 lb. of rye malt
½ lb. of chocolate malt
4 lbs. of gingerbread
½ tsp. of Irish moss
Mash at 155° F for 60 minutes with dried gingerbread.

Gingerbread.

See Brewer's Bread in the Beer Breads section of Part Four, but add one teaspoon each of cloves, ginger, and cinnamon. You'll want to dry out the gingerbread overnight, then add it to the start of the mash.
Boil for 60 minutes.
Add ½ oz. Nugget hops at the 45-minute mark.
Add ½ tsp. of Irish moss at the 15-minute mark.
Add ½ oz. Cascade hops at the 10-minute mark.
Ferment with California Ale yeast or equivalent at 66° F.
OG 1.062
FG 1.016
ABV 6.2
IBU 28
SRM 21

Meados de Santa Claus

This is my Christmas beer release. I tend to alternate years to release it. This beer was a part of Tin Man's grand opening in El Paso. Tin Man labeled it Sun Brewing's Winter Ale, but it was really Meados de Santa Claus. (I think my long beer names throw people off.) This beer has always been a smash hit; it sold out almost immediately at Tin Man. I can't remember if it was three days or three hours but either way it was quick. This beer is essentially Meados de Alien with Christmas-time spices like nutmeg and with darker crystal malts in it.

10 lbs. of American 2-row pale malt
2 lbs. of American crystal malt 80L
6 lbs. of apricots
¼ lb. of red New Mexican chile peppers.
1 tsp. of ground cinnamon.
1 tsp. of ground nutmeg.

Mash at 155° F for 60 minutes.
Mash out at 165° F.
Sparge and Recirculate.

Note: Adding 2 gallons of approximately 190° F will raise the temperature to 165° F.

Boil for 60 minutes.
Add ½ oz. Nugget hops at the 45-minute mark.
Add 1 oz. Ahtanum hops at the 5-minute mark.

Ferment with California Ale yeast or equivalent at 72° F.

Diacetyl Rest: Give a diacetyl rest from the last few days of fermentation while not letting the temperature rise higher than 72° F.

Apricots.

Wash the apricots and add them to a stock pot of water and cook at 140° F for 30 minutes. This ensures all bacteria will be killed. Anything over 102° F will start killing off any bacteria.

Then add it to the secondary fermenter. This is the same concept as dry hopping.

Note: Mashing out at 165 decreases viscosity and it's not hot enough to increase tannins (polyphenols).

OG 1.060
FG 1.014
ABV 6
IBU 26
SRM 16

Award-Winning Beers

Tepache Tamarindo Ale

Winner of the Denver International Gold Medal

This was my first international award-winning beer.

Winning was a very special moment for many reasons. First, Sun Brewing is the smallest brewery in Texas. Second, we won in the Indigenous category, which was a powerful validation of my Borderland Avant-garde style.

Remember, these beers were very radical to the region back then, and Sun Brewing was the only brewery in all of El Paso for quite some time making these types of beers. It gives me pride and joy to see what was once considered radical and extreme become a new normal. I first made Tamarindo Ale and Tepache Ale when I first opened Sun Brewing. I had been making Tepache Tamarindo years before I won the award. Winning was also great recognition for my hard work, blood, sweat, and tears. When you are as small as Sun Brewing, it's easy to feel overlooked. (Expansion is coming! This is just the beginning, ladies and gentlemen. There are very good things coming around the corner for Sun Brewing.)

8 lbs. of Pilsner malt

1 lb. of Munich malt

1 lb. of Victory malt

1 lb. of CaraMunich malt

Tepache (made with tamarind water)

There are a couple steps prior to brewing the beer itself. First, you'll make tamarind water. You'll use that to make tepache, and then you'll use the tepache to make the beer. It's a process, but you won't believe the results!

Tamarind Water.

10 tamarind pods

1 quart of tap water that has been stripped of chlorophenols including chloramine.

1. Peel tamarind pods.
2. Put peeled tamarinds into a pot of water.
3. Bring water to a boil and boil for 15 minutes.
4. Strain tamarinds and all of the seeds.
5. Add ½ tsp. of salt.

Tepache.

Skin of 1 pineapple
Piloncillo, 2 cones of 8 oz.
Tamarind water
2 cinnamon sticks
5 cloves

1. Cut the pineapple skins off the pineapple and rinse them.
2. Place the ingredients in a clay or ceramic pot or Dutch oven with 1 quart of mineral water and 1 quart of tamarind water.
3. Cover clay pot with cheesecloth and let it ferment at room temperature for three days.
4. Strain ingredients out of clay pot, pour the tepache in a pitcher with a lid, and place it in the refrigerator.

Note: This is a 100% spontaneous fermentation. You can let ferment longer than three days, but five days is the longest

I'll let it ferment because each day after five days it starts to taste too much like vinegar.

Now you're ready to brew the beer...

Mash at 149° F for 60 minutes.

Boil for 60 minutes.

Add ½ oz. of Nugget hops at the 45-minute mark.

Take the tepache out of the refrigerator and boil it in a separate pot for 10 minutes, then take it off the heat and let it cool. Once the tepache reaches 65° F, dump it into the fermentation vessel.

Ferment with German ale yeast at 72° F.

Note: Once fermentation begins the temperature can rise significantly, approximately 8° F higher.

OG 1.054

FG 1.014

ABV 5.3

IBU 17

SRM 15

Saison de Membrillo

Winner of the New York (NYIBC) International Silver Medal

I love the attitude of Belgian brewers. They have an anything goes, no rules philosophy that's focused on a flavor profile without limits as opposed to a finite ingredient list. Those rebel brewers of Belgium!

Saison de Membrillo has the classic attributes of a saison:

a citrusy, fruity, spicy, tart, and light malty character that finishes dry.

8 lbs. of Pilsner malt
⅓ lb. of Munich malt
1 lb. of wheat
½ lb. of cane sugar
1.1 oz. Nugget hops
1 lb. 6 oz. of Membrillo

Mash at 150° F for 75 minutes.

Boil for 90 minutes.

Add 0.6 oz. Nugget hops at the 45-minute mark.

Add 4 oz. of Membrillo at the 3-minute mark.

Add ½ oz. Nugget hops and ½ lb. of cane sugar at the 0-minute mark.

Note: Long boils further the reduction of DMS (Dimethyl Sulfide).

Ferment with Belgian saison ale yeast at 72° F. Add 18 oz. of membrillo to the last seven days of fermentation. Approximately the last three days of fermentation, let the temperature rise to no higher than 77° F. The real differentiator for a Belgian saison is truly the yeast. The yeast gives it its character, while the membrillo is subtle in the background.

Note: var Diastaticus for certain types of saison yeast strains can cause contamination. I've had bottles from other saisons that were over-carbonated due to this. I think this probably won't be a problem in the future because we are all getting better at our craft, including yeast manufacturers.

Note: The membrillo was soaked in Mezcal for 30 minutes to sanitize before pitching into fermentation.

Krausening.

Saison de Membrillo is bottle conditioned and krausened. Krausening is a traditional German way of carbonating a beer by introducing a percentage of actively fermenting wort into a batch of beer that has completed fermentation. The active yeast cells from the wort carbonate the batch of beer from the sugars from the malt instead of any additions of outside sugar sources. My recommendation to krausen a beer would be to make two batches of the same beer and use a krausening calculator to achieve the desired volumes of CO_2.

OG 1.051
FG 1.010
ABV 5.4
IBU 20
SRM 4

Trivium Series #3 Charlemagne's Holy Grail

Winner of the New York (NYIBC) International Bronze Medal

To make a beer like this you'll need a lot of passion! It takes a very long brew day and a lot of love and patience. You'll need the Patron Saints of Beer smiling down on you, too, for good fortune, because it's a 100% spontaneous fermentation. Not too many people in Texas or even the entire world brew like this. You have to be a hopeless romantic to even try it.

This is one of the most complex beers I've ever made, and it's a balance of slight tart and slight funk flavor for a full-bodied but very easy drinking beer (though it's over 9 percent ABV).

I was in shock when I first drank it because it didn't taste how I'd expected. I thought the wild yeast would make it more sour and extreme tasting, but it was not extreme at all. It was refreshing and very drinkable for being a high gravity beer. I've made 100% spontaneous ales that had a stronger fusel alcohol bite that were quite estery, but not Charlemagne's.

There are a couple important things to know about this beer before you get going. First, this beer is not filtered and not blended. That's the easy part.

Second, you will have to use a coolship or at least create coolship conditions. If you don't have a homemade coolship, then you could always use your own conical fermenter by opening it up to inoculate. I would call this a conical fermentor coolship. Also, traditionally these beers can only be made in the spring or fall when nighttime temperatures are optimal, generally in the 60-degree range.If you have a cold room, then after inoculation it becomes easy for temperature control.

Third, fermentation takes *at least one year*, so you may want to buy another fermenter so you can keep brewing other beers!

8 lbs. of Pilsner malt

4.5 lbs. of Munich malt 15L

1.7 lbs. of crystal malt 40L

2 lbs. of rye malt

0.8 oz. aged Ahtanum hops (Normally, you don't buy aged hops; consequently, you'll need to age them yourself at room temperature in a dry area. The longer aged, the better).

Do a **one-step mash**:

Beta Amylase Rest at 135 F for 20 minutes

Alpha Amylase Rest at 155 F for 40 minutes

Note: The reason for the single step mash is to add a unique character to the body of the beer that would be difficult to duplicate with single infusion.

Boil for 120 minutes.

Add 0.1 oz. aged Ahtanum hops every 15 minutes.

Note: The long boil is to make the wort more concentrated to extract the thickest, sweetest wort possible for a yearlong fermentation.

Note: It would be a good idea to start buying low alpha acid hops and start aging them. It's not required, but it helps fight bacteria with its antiseptic properties while keeping the IBUs low.

Coolship.

I use a slight modification to the Australian no-chill method to chill the wort before creating coolship conditions for inoculation.

1. Transfer the boiling hot wort to the fermenter and cap it.
2. Turn your cold room to the lowest temperature. By morning, it should be in the proper temperature range, around 60° F. This will take experience to get right but the idea is to cool the wort as fast as you can to the desired fermentation temperature for an ale, which is 60 to 72 degrees. I like the lower end of 60 degrees because I know once the yeast get extremely active the internal temperature raises considerably.
3. Now turn off your cold room and let the wort sit until evening. You're looking for a cool night-time ambient temperature, which for El Paso in October is in the range of 52 to 65° F.
4. Open your fermenter and let it stay open overnight.

5. I cap my fermenter in the morning after approximately 12 hours of being exposed to my brewery's environment for wild yeast and bacteria inoculation.
6. Ferment at 64° F (or at least try to keep it in that range).
7. Monitor your progress over the course of a year, then bottle condition.

My environment is conducive to spontaneous fermentation. I speculate that all the beer and wort spills on the floor and on the walls, promoting yeast and bacteria growth that gets into the air despite how much we clean the place. I also think all the fermentations from past years must be permeating into the walls.

Tips for spontaneous fermentation:

1. If your fermentation gets stuck, then you can keep feeding it by opening up the fermenter for a small amount of time. A few hours should be good, but you can open it up for 6 to 12 hours. These high gravity beers sometimes require it in their years-long journeys.
2. Bottling is a monstrosity. I bottle condition the beers for at least three months and a lot of times six months to a year or longer. The wild yeasts are super aggressive and hard to gauge. Spontaneous ales that I've done have dropped to 1.004 gravity or lower. If you've bottled at 1.008 and it keeps dropping, then you can see it's going to be a Champagne-like bottle opening. I've made the mistake thinking the fermentation was finished and it

was not, so *be sure fermentation is complete before bottling*. Spontaneous ales that drop that low in specific gravity normally have picked up Brettanomyces wild yeast; you will have a very dry beer.

3. Using priming sugar to bottle? If you wanted to try this out, I would use *very little*—approximately 15 percent of what you would normally use. I've had success with priming sugar but also with using nothing.

OG 1.081
FG 1.011
ABV 9.2
IBU less than 7
SRM 15

Beauregard Ice Dark Lager

Winner of the Denver Inaugural Canned Championships - Silver Medal

Beauregard Ice Dark Lager has the classic attributes of an American lager: a clean flavor from the yeast, touches of complex roasted flavors from the chocolate malt and a soft sweet nutty flavor from the Vienna. Very easy drinking beer. When you freeze concentrate this beer, it gives it something special. The icing gives it a different level of smoothness with amplified complexity but it's only a pinch. Excellent beer Beauregard is.

5 lbs. of Pilsner malt
4 lbs. of Vienna malt
.7 lb. of chocolate malt
.7 lb. of Midnight Wheat

Mash at 155° F for 60 minutes.

Sparge and Recirculate.

Boil for 90 minutes.

Add ⅓ oz. Nugget hops at the 45-minute mark.

Ferment at 50° F with American Lager yeast or other clean yeast for at least a month. Then transfer to secondary for at least another month of lagering.

Note: As with all my beers, even my lagers, this is bottle conditioned.

Diacetyl Rest: Give a diacetyl rest to 65° F for at least three days.

Freeze distillation, also known as freeze concentration, basically means that you are freezing water out of your finished beer to reduce it by a percentage, therefore concentrating the alcohol.

If you have a 5-gallon batch of beer that is 5 percent ABV

and you freeze the entire 5 gallons and reduce it by half, then you would have doubled the concentration, meaning you would have taken the beer from 5 percent ABV to 10 percent. I don't freeze entire batches. A 10–20 percent concentration is good enough. This not only concentrates the beer, it amplifies the taste.

In this case, I reduce 20 percent by half, which raises the ABV by 1 point. Consequently, I went from a 5 percent beer to a 6 percent beer.

Refer to Working Man Ice Ale for ice procedure.

OG 1.051

FG 1.013

ABV 5 plus one ABV point after freeze concentration to equal 6 abv.

IBU 10

SRM 22

Quintessential Borderland Avant-garde Ales.

Technically, almost all my beers have at least a hint of the borderlands in them, but these beers best express my culinary fusion and vision for borderland avant-garde cuisine. BAG beer can be almost any style even beers with only 4 ingredients if they're indigenous or spontaneous. I believe taking beer to that next level of flavor would involve making beers that have an indigenous taste and feel to them even if it's malting your own grains or culturing your own yeast strain for a unique local flavor profile.

Tepache Sour Ale

This beer is a derivative of Tepache Ale that uses kettle souring.

I've been making tepache since my first day in business; it's a beverage I fell in love with in the parks of Mexico. Tepache is a beautiful blend of sweet, sour, and spice; it's absolutely magnificent in every way, and now, together with Tepache Ale, my favorite beverage.

5.5 lbs. of American 2-row pale malt
1 lb. of crystal malt 20L
32 oz. of Tepache (See Beverages in Part Four)
Mash at 153° F for 60 minutes.

Kettle Sour.

Wash the rinds of three pineapples. Then dump them into the boil kettle with the wort and cover it with a cheese cloth. Let it sit for 12 hours, then continue to the boil.
Boil for 60 minutes.
Add ⅓ oz. Nugget hops at the 45-minute mark.
Ferment with Belgian Saison Ale yeast at 72° F until approximately the last three days of the fermentation, then let it rise no higher than 77° F.
Add tepache to the secondary fermentation.
OG 1.033
FG 1.008
ABV 3.2
IBU 17

SRM 5

Tepache IPA

This beer is a hoppy tart of a beer. The goal was to have a hoppy beer like an IPA as a base beer then to infuse the flavors of tepache and sour it.

The key to this beer, as with a lot of beers, is balance. You'll want to avoid souring the beer so much it overpowers the base beer or the tepache. This is really more to taste, but for me you'll need to adjust how sour your tepache is and take it up a notch or two because the taste mellows out from the brewing process. You can adjust how much volume of tepache you use based on how sour your tepache is. I taste my tepache every day to monitor the sourness.

10 lbs. of American 2-row malt

1 lb. of crystal malt 15L

32 oz. of tepache (see Tepache Tamarindo Ale or Beverages in Part Four)

Mash at 153° F for 60 minutes.

Kettle Sour.

Wash the rinds of three pineapples. Then dump them into the boil kettle with the wort and cover it with a cheese cloth. Let it sit for 12 hours, then continue to the boil.

Boil for 60 minutes.

Add ½ oz. Simcoe hops at the 45-minute mark.

Add ½ oz. Simcoe hops at the 30-minute mark.

Add ½ oz. Cascade hops at the 15-minute mark.

Add ½ oz. Cascade hops at the 0-minute mark.

Ferment with California Ale yeast or equivalent at 72° F.

Add Tepache to the secondary fermentation.

Dry hop the last five days of secondary fermentation. The best hops to use for this are strong aroma and flavor hops.

OG 1.060

FG 1.014

ABV 6

IBU 45

SRM 5

Tamarindo Ale

Tamarindo Ale is one of the most beloved beers that I've made in this region; it even rivals Meados de Alien!

I've made this beer in several ways—even with tamarindo Mexican candy, which gives it a unique ruby red hue. I made Tamarindo Ale when I first opened Sun Brewing and was trying to introduce my borderland avant-garde style to El Paso.

This recipe was probably my second or third recipe and is a straightforward approach to brewing tamarindo ale.

8 lbs. of American 2-row pale malt
1.3 lb. of Munich malt
½ lb. of crystal malt 40L
½ lb. of crystal malt 120L
2 lbs. of tamarinds
Mash at 155° F for 60 minutes.
Boil for 60 minutes.
Add ½ oz. Nugget hops at the 45-minute mark.
Add 2 lbs. Tamarinds at the 10-minute mark.
Note: You'll need to peel and wash the tamarinds.
Ferment with California Ale yeast or equivalent at 72° F.
OG 1.052
FG 1.011
ABV 5.4
IBU 22
SRM 16

Tamarindo Porter

This beer is a natural continuation of my exploration of Tamarindo Ales. This is one of my all-time favorite porters! It's slightly bittersweet with a touch of tart from the tamarinds. To take it up a notch, brew it with tamarind water!

8 lbs. of American 2-row pale malt
1 lb. of brown malt
1 lb. of crystal malt 80L
1 lb. of chocolate malt
2 lbs. of tamarinds
Mash at 155° F for 60 minutes.
Boil for 60 minutes.
Add ½ oz. Nugget hops at the 45-minute mark.
Add 2 lbs. tamarinds at the 10-minute mark.
Note: You'll need to peel and wash the tamarinds.
Ferment with California Ale yeast or equivalent at 66° F.
OG 1.053
FG 1.012
ABV 5.4
IBU 22

This picture was taken at Tosca Stone Oven Pizzeria. Before it closed, they carried some half dozen of our beers. Gustavo and Serge were great partners in the Sun Brewing story.

Chamoy Ale

This beer made perfect sense to me because of the popularity of **clamato** and **michelada** drinks. Chamoy has grown in popularity over the years, especially with the explosion of social media, but I remember not too long ago not a lot of people that I ran across knew what chamoy was.

Chamoy is one of my all-time favorite sauces; I use it all the time. Chamoy is a salty, spicy, sweet, and sour sauce, and can liven up a beer with an exquisite unique taste.

I believe one day this beer will win an award. It's just got to find its audience.

9 lbs. of American 2-row pale malt
1 lb. of Munich malt
1 lb. of crystal malt 60L
½ lb. of chamoy (See Sauces in Part Four)
Mash at 153° F for 60 minutes.
Sparge and Recirculate.
Boil for 60 minutes.

Add ½ oz. Nugget hops at the 45-minute mark.
Add ½ lb. of chamoy at the 5-minute mark.
Ferment with California Ale yeast or equivalent at 66° F.
OG 1.055
FG 1.014
ABV 5.4
IBU 22
SRM 13

Huitlacoche Wildflower Ale

Huitlacoche is a fungus that grows on corn, but it is also a real delicacy. It is earthy and mushroom-like while still silky and smooth. This is awesomeness in a beer. Huitlacoche gives the beer an earthy, umami undertone.

9 lbs. of American 2-row pale malt
1 lb. of crystal malt 15L
3 lbs. of huitlacoche
Mash at 153° F for 60 minutes.
Boil for 60 minutes.
Add ⅓ oz. Nugget hops at the 45-minute mark.
Add 1 lb. of Huitlacoche at the 5-minute mark.
Ferment with California Ale yeast or equivalent at 72° F.
Wash the rest of the huitlacoche and add them to a stock pot with 140° F water for 30 minutes. This ensures all bacteria will be killed. Anything over 102° F will start killing off any bacteria. Add huitlacoche to the secondary fermenter.

Note: When you add huitlacoche to the boil, it will kill off any bacteria, so this step is only necessary for the huitlacoche added to the fermenter.

OG 1.050
FG 1.013
ABV 5
IBU 14
SRM 5

Green Mole Ale

Not just another mole beer! Green Mole is slightly tart, herbal, and spicy. This beer usually has head-retention problems, but it tastes really good. You can customize your green mole, of course. Think of it like a stew taco shop needs custom tortillas to accommodate their soupy tacos. It's the same concept here in order to get a similar flavor profile without your beer being killed from the oils.

You can ruin a batch of beer with too much oil. It will be drinkable, but not many people are going to want to drink a beer that is oily from mole. To alleviate this problem, I substitute broth for beer when making the mole. This makes a good beer with a green mole undertone and minimal head retention problems and oils from the mole.

9 lbs. of American 2-row pale malt
1 lb. of crystal malt 15L
½ lb. of Green Mole (see Sauces in Part Four)
Mash at 154° F for 60 minutes.
Sparge and Recirculate.

Boil for 60 minutes.
Add ½ oz. Nugget hops at the 45-minute mark.
Add ½ lb. of Green Mole at the 5-minute mark.
Ferment with California Ale yeast or equivalent at 66° F.
OG 1.050
FG 1.013
ABV 5
IBU 14
SRM 5

Atole Breakfast Stout

Atole is a very special and beloved beer. The addition of **atole** doesn't produce that exact flavor so much as it creates a mouthfeel coupled with atole spice. The name has a lot to do with its popularity because for people who love atole, the name alone conjures up sweet cultural memories.

I've made this beer in a few different ways, including as a milk stout. You just add 1 lb. of lactose (milk sugar) either late in the boil or during primary fermentation. This will sweeten things up. Both ways are very good! I prefer the milk stout version for my Beer-Nuts Cereal (see Part Four)!

7 lbs. of American 2-row pale
1 lb. of American crystal malt 80L
½ lb. of chocolate malt
½ lb. of Black Patent malt
32 oz. of atole (see Beverages in Part Four)
Mash at 155° F for 60 minutes.
Boil for 60 minutes.

Add ⅓ oz. Nugget hops at the 45-minute mark.
Add 32 oz. of Atole at the 15-minute mark.
Ferment with California Ale yeast or equivalent at 66° F.
OG 1.044
FG 1.011
ABV 4.3
IBU 16
SRM 34

Vagabundo Ale

This beer encompasses a lot of the flavors I made in other beers; I wanted to combine my favorite flavors into one beer and see what happened. Think Jamaica, Mexican chocolate, and chile, a slightly sour citrusy, spicy, nutty, chocolatey, and sweet brewski. A complexity to die for…

9 lbs. of American 2-row pale malt
½ lb. of crystal malt 40L
½ lb. of crystal malt 120L
⅓ lb. of chocolate malt
3 oz. of orange zest
3 oz. of hibiscus
⅓ lb. of Abuelita Mexican chocolate
⅓ oz. of Achiote chile
Mash at 155° F for 60 minutes.
Sparge and Recirculate.
Boil for 60 minutes.
Add ½ oz. Nugget hops at the 45-minute mark.
⅓ lb. of Mexican chocolate at the 20-minute mark.

Add 3 oz. of hibiscus at the 10-minute mark.
Add 3 oz. of orange zest at the 5-minute mark.
Add ⅓ oz. of Achiote chile at the 3-minute mark.
Ferment with California Ale yeast or equivalent at 66° F.
OG 1.049
FG 1.011
ABV 5
IBU 15
SRM 15

Nicodemus Ale

Nicodemus is a great beer to bake bread with and cook with. On a cool autumn afternoon, with the leaves falling, it's great to have a Nicodemus Ale with some rustic beer bread.

Nicodemus has a slight and balanced biscuity, nutty, citrusy, spicy, and malty flavor that finishes smooth. A great multi-purpose beer.

8 lbs. of American 2-row pale malt
1 lbs. of Munich malt

1 lbs. of Vienna malt
½ lb. of crystal malt 80L
1 oz. of Canutillo lemon zest
⅓ oz. of sage
Mash at 155° F for 60 minutes.
Boil for 60 minutes.
Add ½ oz. Nugget hops at the 45-minute mark.
Add 1 oz. of lemon zest at the 5-minute mark.
Add ⅓ oz. of sage at the 3-minute mark.
Ferment with California Ale yeast or equivalent at 66° F.
OG 1.052
FG 1.013
ABV 5.1
IBU 14
SRM 12

Gypsies' Brew

Roses give this beer a unique and striking flavor. Hierba de Vibora (green tea) takes a back seat and is subtle. The roses give the beer a very pleasant, sweet, tart, herbal taste, unlike most herbs and spices, while the amaranth grains give the beer an earthy, grainy undertone. I germinated the grains for five days.

This beer is very refreshing and tastes great in the summertime. I really love the flavor of this beer, and it's my wife's favorite of all time. When I released this beer, I paired it with an amaranth beer-breaded steak.

8 lbs. of American 2-row pale malt

3 lbs. of amaranth grain
½ lb. of crystal malt 60L
3 oz.s of Hierba de Vibora
32 oz. of roses
Mash at 155° F for 60 minutes.

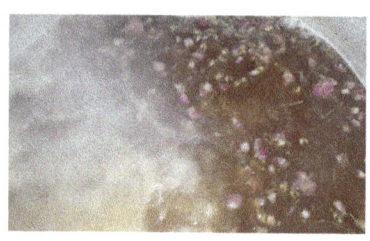

Boil for 60 minutes.
Add ½ oz. Nugget hops at the 45-minute mark.
Add 32 oz. of roses at the 15-minute mark.
Add 3 oz. of Hierba de Vibora at the 5-minute mark.
Ferment with California Ale yeast or equivalent at 70° F.
OG 1.050
FG 1.013
ABV 5
IBU 15
SRM 5

Gypsies' Beer Music Gruit

I wanted to get medieval on this beer. Before hops, European brewers used an herb mixture called gruit. No recipes survive, just references here and there, so it's always a guess when you're making it, but it's a fun way to go back in time—and it tastes good, too!

The high amount of lemons works as a preservative, but this beer was meant to drink right away.

The beer has an herbal lemon-lime taste, with a dry, slightly caramel finish.

1½ lbs. of American 2-row pale malt

1.5 lb. of crystal malt 60L

12 oz. of Hierba de Vibora

6 oz. of lemon zest

3 oz. of lemon juice

3 oz. of local honey

1 oz. of sage

1 oz. of cilantro

Mash at 155° F for 60 minutes.

Boil for 60 minutes.

Add ½ oz. Nugget hops at the 45-minute mark.

Add 32 oz. of roses at the 15-minute mark.

Add 3 oz. of Hierba de Vibora at the 5-minute mark.

Ferment with California Ale yeast or equivalent at 70° F.

OG 1.063

FG 1.015

ABV 6.3

IBU 14

SRM 12

Mesquite Bean Ale

I made this in my first six months of business. Bean pods

give it a unique smokey-sweet taste, but it has the malt forwardness of an amber ale. I had only been open maybe a few months when I made this beer, and I paired it with mesquite bean-flour bread items. I baked the mesquite bean pods, then ground them through my mill to turn it into flour for making rustic bread and mesquite bean tortillas.

8 lbs. of American 2-row pale malt
1 lb. of Victory malt
½ lb. of crystal malt 15L
½ lb. of crystal malt 80L
1 lb. of mesquite beans
Mash at 155° F for 60 minutes.

Mesquite Bean Preparation.

Wash your mesquite bean pods. In my case there are mesquite bean trees everywhere, including right next to the brewery. I smoke the mesquite beans with mesquite wood chunks on low heat until softened, usually a couple of hours on indirect heat, with a water pan underneath filled with beer.

Boil for 60 minutes.
Add ½ oz. Nugget hops at the 45-minute mark.
Add 1 lb. of mesquite bean pods at the 15-minute mark.
Ferment with California Ale yeast or equivalent at 72° F.
OG 1.050
FG 1.010
ABV 5.3
IBU 25
SRM 10

Meados de Alien Lager

The clean, crisp quality from the lager yeast serves as a great body for the mild, apricot-fruity flavors with a touch of warmness from the chile peppers.

9 lbs. of American 2-row pale
1 lb. of acid malt
1 lb. of Carapils malt
1 lb. of American crystal malt 60L
4 lbs. of apricots
¼ lb. of red New Mexican chile peppers

Mash at 153° F for 90 minutes to ensure complete conversion.

Sparge and Recirculate.

Boil for 90 minutes to reduce DMS.

Add ⅓ oz. Nugget hops at the 45-minute mark.

Add ⅓ oz. Simcoe hops at the 15-minute mark.

Ferment at 50° F with American Lager yeast for at least a month. Then transfer to secondary for at least another month of lagering.

Add apricot puree to the last week of secondary fermentation. See Meados de Alien Ale for how to make the puree.

Note: As with all my beers, even my lagers, this is bottle conditioned.

Diacetyl Rest: Give a diacetyl rest to 65° F for three days.

OG 1.058
FG 1.013
ABV 5.9
IBU 20

SRM 9

Green Chamoy Pickle Sour Lager

This lager is spectacular! It sounds like it will be too much, but the flavor really isn't as striking as it sounds. It has a classic, clean, crisp lager feel that is malt forward to balance the undertone of spice and sourness. I've been experimenting with sour lagers and I think lagers make the very best sour beers in the entire world!

8 lbs. of American 2-row pale malt
1 lb. of ccid malt
1 lb. of Carapils malt
0.8 lb. of American crystal malt 80L
1 lb. of Victory malt

Mash at 153° F for 90 minutes to ensure complete conversion.

Sparge and Recirculate.

Add a pint of Green Chamoy Pickle sauce to the boil kettle and cover with a cheese cloth. Let it sit overnight.

Boil for 90 minutes to reduce DMS.

Add ⅓ oz. Nugget hops at the 45-minute mark.

Add ⅓ oz. Mosaic hops at the 15-minute mark.

Ferment at 50° F with American Lager yeast for at least a month. Then transfer to secondary for at least another month of lagering.

Add a pint of green chamoy pickle sauce to the last week of secondary fermentation.

Note: As with all my beers, even my lagers, this is bottle conditioned.

Diacetyl Rest: Give a diacetyl rest to 65° F for three days.

OG 1.057

FG 1.014

ABV 5.6

IBU 20

SRM 12

100% Spontaneous Ales.

My spontaneous ales are uniquely American but are inspired by true Belgian lambics. These beers can also be BAG

(Borderland Avant-garde) too because of the indigenous nature of the beer. Normally, my 100% Spontaneous Ales only have 4 ingredients, water, barley, hops and wild yeast. Actually, five ingredients if you include everything the beer is inoculated with which would include wild bacteria like lactobacillus. This is a BAG beer because the local microbes from the air that inoculate the beer give it a unique indigenous borderland flavor that would be impossible to duplicate.

100% Spontaneous Ale Brewing Helpful Hints

Though the fermentation is spontaneous, it shouldn't surprise you that there is a certain amount of planning and foresight involved. You'll invest a lot of time and even space in your home to this beer, so you want to set yourself up for success.

Cleaning and Sanitation

This is the exact same as regular brewing. Clean and sanitize everything. Inoculations come from the bacteria and microbes from the air in your ambient environment.

Boiling Wort

You are going to want very long boil times to concentrate the wort as much as you can to sustain the long fermentation. Boil for a minimum of 90 minutes.

Fermentation Temperature

Keep it in the normal ale range. I normally target the mid-60-degree range, between 65 and 67 but no higher than 72° F. You want your flavors to come from the wild yeast and bacteria. Brettanomyces lambicus is a common wild yeast strain responsible for a lot of unique flavors such as barnyard funk and spice. It also has a tendency to drop the final gravity to very low and sometimes to zero.

Coolships

You could build your own custom coolship but make it shallow so that the air has the maximum exposure to the wort to cool and inoculate the wort. One idea to build a coolship would be to cut a metal keg in half. If you have no coolship then open up your fermenter to accomplish what a coolship is for, which is to inoculate and cool the wort.

Method.

I use a slight modification to the Australian no-chill method.

1. Transfer the boiling hot wort to the fermenter and cap it.
2. Turn your cold room to the lowest temperature until proper temperature range, between 60–72° F.
3. Now turn off your cold room and let the wort sit until

evening. You're looking for a cool night-time ambient temperature, which for El Paso in October is in the range of 52 to 65° F.
4. Open your fermenter and let it stay open overnight.
5. I cap my fermenter in the morning after approximately 12 hours of being exposed to my brewery's environment for wild yeast and bacteria inoculation.
6. Ferment at 64° F (or at least try to keep it in that range).
7. Monitor your progress over the course of a year, then bottle condition.

My environment is conducive to spontaneous fermentation. I speculate that all the beer and wort spills on the floor and on the walls, promoting yeast and bacteria growth that gets into the air despite how much we clean the place. I also think all the fermentations from past years must be permeating into the walls.

Tips for spontaneous fermentation:

1. If your fermentation gets stuck, then you can keep feeding it by opening up the fermenter for a small amount of time. A few hours should be good, but you can open it up for 6 to 12 hours. These high gravity beers sometimes require it in their years-long journeys.
2. Bottling is a monstrosity. I bottle condition the beers for at least three months and a lot of times six months to a year. The wild yeasts are super aggressive and hard to gauge. Spontaneous ales that I've done have

dropped to 1.004 gravity. If you've bottled at 1.008 and it keeps dropping, then you can see it's going to be a Champagne-like bottle opening. I've made the mistake thinking the fermentation was finished and it was not, so *be sure fermentation is complete before bottling*. Spontaneous ales that drop that low in specific gravity normally have picked up Brettanomyces wild yeast; you will have a very dry beer.

Using priming sugar to bottle? If you wanted to try this out, I would use *very little*—approximately 15 percent of what you would normally use. I've had success with priming sugar but also with using nothing.

Mold

If you get mold, it's because of moisture built up after you've capped your fermenters. You need to catch this immediately and scrape it off the top. If you didn't catch this immediately—meaning within 24 hours—then dump the batch.

Normally mold can't contaminate beer because of the alcohol content. Blue, green, and white molds won't present a problem if you catch them early. Scrape them off and move on. However, if the mold is any color other than blue, green, or white, then dump the batch; it's contaminated and even dangerous to ingest. I also dump any batch that has too much mold. If you have just a small spot or two, then it's easy to scrape it off the top with a sterilized ladle. Some molds in fermentation are normal in the food making process, like with blue cheese and sauerkraut, but it's not desirable in brewing beer.

Off Flavors

Essentially, there are three phases to making a 100% spontaneous ale. In the initial four months, your primary fermentation should be coming to a close or have finished. You'll see all the bubblies in the first phase just like a cultured yeast fermentation.

The second four months, your beer will taste bad or not so good. *Don't dump the beer!* I don't know how many times I wanted to dump a batch of spontaneous beer thinking it was bad when really it was just cleaning itself up.

The final phase is when your beer is mostly cleaned up and starting to taste good. Remember, 100% spontaneous ales are the ultimate in romantic brewing. They're like a fine wine that just gets better with age.

100% spontaneous ales are truly unique, and even expert beer judges have a difficult time grading beers as complex as these. Ultimately, if you like it, then it's good. One person's treasure is another person's trash.

Recipes

Beyond the Pale

A 100% spontaneous IPA

This beer is something I dreamed up because I was thinking to myself; "American IPAs are basically bold bitterness with American hop flavor and aroma. To achieve the flavor and aroma, it's basically all dry hopping."

That's when the light bulb went off in my head. I can achieve the beautiful complexities of a 100% spontaneous ale with just the right amount of bitterness coupled with the dry-hopped flavor and aroma!

This beer is not filtered and not blended.

12 lbs. of American 2-row pale malt

1 lb. of crystal malt 120L

1 lb. of rye malt

One step mash:

Beta Amylase rest at 135° F for 20 minutes

Alpha Amylase rest at 155° F for 40 minutes

Boil for 120 minutes.

Add oz. El Dorado hops at 120-minute mark.

Add oz. Ahtanum hops 90-minute mark.

Add .1 oz. Ahtanum hops every 15 minutes from the 75-minute mark.

Dry hop the last five days of fermentation with 3 oz. of Ahtanum.

Note: These hops are not aged.

Ferment according to coolship instructions above.

OG 1.070

FG 1.004

ABV 8.6

IBU 40

SRM 14

100% Spontaneous Tepache Ale.

This beer is not filtered and not blended.
9 lbs. of American 2-row pale malt
1 lb. of crystal malt 60L
64 ounces of tepache (see Beverages in Part Four)
One step mash:
Beta Amylase Rest 135° F for 20 minutes
Alpha Amylase Rest 155° F for 40 minutes
Boil for 120 minutes.
Add 0.1 oz. of El Dorado hops at the 120-minute mark.
Add 0.1 oz. of Ahtanum hops at the 60-minute mark.
Add 0.1 oz. of Ahtanum hops at the 45-minute mark.
Add 0.1 oz. of Ahtanum hops at the 15-minute mark.
Add tepache at the 3-minute mark.
Ferment according to coolship instructions above.
OG 1.050
FG 1.004
ABV 6
IBU 12
SRM 9

100% Spontaneous 6th Anniversary Tamale Top Ale.

This beer is not filtered and not blended.
8 lbs. of American 2-row pale malt

1 lb. of American crystal 60L malt
1 lb. of American chocolate malt 350L
6 lbs. of 6th Anniversary Sweet Tamales (see Part Four)

One step mash:
Add 6 lbs. of dried sweet tamales at beginning of mash.
Beta Amylase Rest 135° F for 20 minutes
Alpha Amylase Rest 155° F for 40 minutes
Sparge and Recirculate.

Boil for 120 minutes.
Add 0.1 oz. of Nugget hops at the 120-minute mark.
Add 0.1 oz. of aged Ahtanum hops at the 60-minute mark.
Add 0.1 oz. of aged Ahtanum hops at the 45-minute mark.
Add 0.1 oz. of aged Ahtanum hops at the 15-minute mark.

Ferment according to coolship instructions above.
OG 1.053
FG 1.010
ABV 5.6
IBU 12
SRM 30

Illegitame non Carborundum.

A 100% spontaneous ale.
This beer is not filtered and not blended.

My friend, Joe the Marine JAG officer, gave me the idea for the name for this beer. I've also made this beer refermented with cherries.

6 lbs. of American 2-row pale malt
1.5 lbs. of American crystal malt 40L

1 lb. of American chocolate malt 350L
2 lbs. of rye malt.
One step Mash:
Beta Amylase Rest 135 F for 20 minutes
Alpha Amylase Rest 155 F for 40 minutes
Sparge and Recirculate.
Boil for 120 minutes.
Add 0.1 oz. of Nugget hops at the 120-minute mark.
Add 0.1 oz. of aged Ahtanum hops at the 60-minute mark.
Add 0.1 oz. of aged Ahtanum hops at the 45-minute mark.
Add 0.1 oz. of aged Ahtanum hops at the 15-minute mark.
Ferment according to coolship instructions above.
OG 1.052
FG 1.006
ABV 6.0
IBU 11
SRM 30

My Weird Beers.

The Fozzie Lime Stout

I was the weirdo who would take a small lime wedge and squeeze it in my stout. I would do this a lot back in the old days before I was a student of beer. I still do it from time to time and I like the sweet and sour taste of it coupled with the coffee and roasty flavor of a stout.

The goal here is to make a stout with a little sweetness

and to complement it with a little sourness. We achieve the sweetness by not having a striking flavor to overpower it, for example, not making this beer too bitter or dry. We avoid dryness by not adding any adjuncts like sugar for having a higher ABV but with crystal malts which makes it sweeter.

This was one of the very first stouts I made at Sun Brewing. It was pretty radical back then, and it is still pretty radical today.

I think people's tastes and perceptions are changing over time. I've always thought a stout could be refreshing on a beach, however you would have to associate a refreshing beverage encompassing roasty and chocolatey flavors on a warm sunny day.

This stout makes a refreshing drink on the beach with flavors of sweet, sour, coffee, and chocolate undertones.

6.3 lbs. of American 2-row pale malt
1 lb. of American crystal malt 40L
1 lb. of American crystal malt 120L
½ lb. of chocolate malt
½ lb. of black patent malt
1.5 oz. of lime zest
1.5 oz. of lime juice

Mash at 155° F for 60 minutes.
Boil for 60 minutes.
Add ⅓ oz. Nugget hops at the 45-minute mark.
Add 1.5 oz. of lime zest at the 5-minute mark.
Add 1.5 oz. of freshly squeezed lime juice at the 3-minute mark.
Ferment with California Ale yeast or equivalent at 66° F.

OG 1.045
FG 1.011
ABV 4.4
IBU 16
SRM 37

Avocado Sour Ale

This beer is a derivative of my original Avocado Ale. I made Avocado Ale in my first year in business. It was a major experiment, as I'm sure you can imagine.

Avocados have a rich buttery and decadent flavor that is not overpowering. It's truly a magnificent, rich, and savory fruit, however, when it comes to beer it does not produce a striking flavor.

That's okay, because when you brew with adjuncts, you're not trying to have that exact flavor so much as to see what the consequence of using that adjunct is. In my avocado ales, I get more of a mouthfeel and texture added to the beer while the flavor is only slightly affected.

Using avocados will give you a head-retention problem; it would be difficult to win a technical award for this beer, but it tastes great! The avocados complement the sourness and give the beer a unique mouthfeel.

7 lbs. of American 2-row pale malt
1 lb. of American crystal malt 15L
5 lbs. of avocados
Skins of three pineapples.
Mash at 153° F for 60 minutes.

Kettle Sour.

Dump the pineapple rinds into the boil kettle with the wort and cover it with a cheese cloth.

Let it sit overnight, then continue to the boil. If you want it sourer, you can kettle sour the wort for longer. I recommend not going over three days because the sourness can start to get too strong or have a vinegar taste.

Boil for 60 minutes.

Add ⅓ oz. Nugget hops at the 45-minute mark.

Avocado Preparation.

Wash and peel the avocados. Extract the oils from the avocados by heating them in water at 140° F for about 30 minutes until the oils begin seeping out. This also ensures all bacteria will be killed. Anything over 102° F will start killing off any bacteria.

Ferment with California Ale yeast or equivalent at 66° F.

Add avocados to the secondary fermenter. This is the same concept as dry hopping.

OG 1.040

FG 1.010

ABV 4

IBU 16

SRM 5

Vertigo Ale

The goal of this American specialty ale was to have mild bitterness and Kona coffee flavors instead of a typical ale's strong hop aromas and flavors. I don't make this beer much, anymore, but it remains a personal favorite.

8 lbs. of American 2-row pale malt
1.5 lbs. of Victory malt
1.5 lbs. of crystal malt 80L
Mash at 155° F for 60 minutes.
Boil for 60 minutes.
Add ½ oz. Nugget hops at the 45-minute mark.
Ferment with California Ale yeast or equivalent at 72° F.
Dry hop the last three days of fermentation with 4 oz. of Kona coffee beans.

OG 1.054
FG 1.014
ABV 5.3
IBU 22
SRM 16

Nirvana Russian Kvas Ale

7 lbs. of American 2-row pale malt
3 lbs. of rye malt
32 oz. of Russian Kvas (see Beverages in Part Four)
Mash at 155° F for 60 minutes.
Boil for 60 minutes.
Add ⅓ oz. Nugget hops at the 45-minute mark.

Ferment with Belgium Saison Ale yeast at 72° F until approximately the last three days of the fermentation, then let it rise no higher than 77° F.

Add Russian Kvas to the secondary fermentation.

OG 1.050
FG 1.013
ABV 4.8
IBU 17
SRM 4

Green Chamoy Pickle Ale

8 lbs. of American 2-row pale malt
1.5 lb. of crystal malt 20L
16 oz. of Green Chamoy (see Sauces in Part Four)
3 pickles

Mash at 155° F for 60 minutes.

Sparge and Recirculate.

Boil for 60 minutes.

Add ⅓ oz. Nugget hops at the 45-minute mark.

Add ⅓ oz. Cascade hops at the 10-minute mark.

Add 32 oz. of chamoy sauce and pickles at the 5-minute mark.

Ferment with California Ale yeast or equivalent at 72° F.

OG 1.048
FG 1.012
ABV 4.7
IBU 19
SRM 6

DAVID SLOCUM

Symposius Sour Porter

This is a classic porter... soured. I always thought a porter/stout type of beer would taste great with some sourness—and it does! I envisioned a refreshing porter in the summertime watching the ball game in the stadium, kickin' it with a good stadium dog or beer brat.

7.5 lbs. of American 2-row pale malt
1 lb. of chocolate malt
1 lb. of Victory Malt
½ lb. of crystal malt 80L
½ lb. of roasted barley malt
Skins from 3 pineapples.
Mash at 153° F for 60 minutes.

Kettle Sour.

Dump the pineapple rinds into the boil kettle with the wort and cover it with a cheese cloth.

Let it sit for 24 hours, then continue to the boil. Depending on how sour you want this beer, you can kettle sour the wort for longer. I recommend not going over three days because the sourness can start to get too strong and even have a vinegar taste.

Boil for 60 minutes.
Add ⅓ oz. Nugget hops at the 45-minute mark.
Add ⅓ oz. Ahtanum hops at the 10-minute mark.
Ferment with California Ale yeast or equivalent at 67° F.
OG 1.051

FG 1.013
ABV 5
IBU 17
SRM 37

Narama Ancho Chile Sour Ale

I named this beer after Narama, a Cora Indian saint and the patron of salt, mezcal, and chiles. The concept of this beer is to have a malty beer with a touch of chile spice complemented with a soured beer.

I wanted to create a very unique beer that sour beer lovers would embrace because of the balance of the malt sweetness and the grain bill's complexity coupled with the mild, sweet, and smoky flavor of the ancho chile.

10 lbs. of American 2-row pale malt
2 lb. of Munich malt
1 lb. of Victory malt
1 lb. of crystal malt 80L
½ lb. of chocolate malt
½ lb. of ancho chiles
Skins from 3 pineapples.
Mash at 155° F for 60 minutes.
Sparge and Recirculate.

Kettle Sour.

Dump the pineapple rinds into the boil kettle with the wort and cover it with a cheese cloth.

Let it sit for 48 hours, then continue to the boil. You can sour it longer if you want a stronger sour flavor. I recommend not going over three days, however, because the sourness can start to get a vinegar taste.

Boil for 60 minutes.

Add ⅓ oz. Nugget hops at the 45-minute mark.

Add ⅓ oz. Citra hops at the 10-minute mark.

Ancho Chile Preparation.

Wash and seed the ancho chiles. Put the chiles in a pot with water and heat to at least 140° F for 30 minutes. This ensures all bacteria will be killed. Anything over 102° F will start killing off any bacteria.

Ferment with California Ale yeast or equivalent at 70° F.

Strain the ancho chiles and add them to the secondary fermenter. This is the same concept as dry hopping.

OG 1.071

FG 1.018

ABV 6.9

IBU 17

SRM 29

Swords & Ale

As with most of the beers in this cookbook, this is another beer from my first year in business. This was one of my first wild ales, and it came out biscuit, bready, nutty, chocolatey, funky, and tart. In other words, lovely!

10 lbs. of American 2-row pale malt
1 lb. of Victory malt
1 lb. of crystal malt 60L
½ lb. of chocolate malt
½ lb. of hibiscus
½ lb. of Abuelita Mexican chocolate
Mash at 155° F for 60 minutes.
Sparge and Recirculate.

Kettle Coolship.

Leave open the boil kettle with the wort and cover it with a cheese cloth.

Let it sit for 24 hours, then continue to the boil. With wild ales there is no telling which way the beer could go... maybe it turns out a little on the sour side, or maybe it's not sour at all. Normally, when I do a wild ale, it has a little funk and very little sourness.

Boil for 60 minutes.
Add ⅓ oz. Nugget hops at the 45-minute mark.
Add ½ lb. of Abuelita Mexican chocolate at the 30-minute mark.
Add hibiscus flowers at the 20-minute mark.
Add ⅓ oz. Ahtanum hops at the 10-minute mark.
Ferment with California Ale yeast or equivalent at 66° F.
OG 1.062
FG 1.013
ABV 6.4
IBU 16

SRM 22

Wasshoppening Wild Malt Liquor

6.5 lbs. of American 2-row pale malt
1 lb. of crystal malt 10L
1 lb. of Carapils malt
4 lbs. of chicales
⅓ lb. of local honey

Cereal Mash.

This is a separate mash from the all-grain mash. You can do this in a stock pot on the stove.

1. Rinse and clean the chicales.
2. Fill a 5-gallon pot with three gallons of purified water.
3. Put the chicales in the pot and heat on low to medium heat.
4. Stir the chicales every few minutes or so.
5. Bring the water to 155° F, then hold for 15 minutes.
6. Then turn the heat up until the water boils.
7. Boil for 30 minutes while stirring frequently.

Main Mash.

Mash at 155° F for 60 minutes.
Dump the chicales in sometime in the first 15 minutes.
Mash out at 165° F.

Sparge and Recirculate.

Inoculate wort with wild things in a boil kettle by opening it up to the air and covering it with cheese cloth for at least a day. I normally don't go over 3 days. This is also to taste; taste the wort to see if it reaches the complexities you're looking for.

Boil for 90 minutes.

Add ⅓ oz. Nugget hops at the 45-minute mark.

Add ⅓ lb. of honey at the 1-minute mark.

Ferment with California Ale yeast or equivalent at 62° F.

Diacetyl Rest: Give a diacetyl rest from the last few days of fermentation while not letting the temperature rise higher than 70° F.

OG 1.066
FG 1.016
ABV 6.6
IBU 16
SRM 4

Le Cygne Noir Black Saison

th

8 lbs. of Pilsner malt
1 lb. of Munich malt
0.7 lb. of Midnight Wheat
½ lb. of cane sugar
3 oz. of orange zest
1 tsp. of cilantro
1 tsp. of sage

Mash at 150° F for 75 minutes.
Sparge and Recirculate.
Boil for 90 minutes.
Add ⅓ oz. Nugget hops at the 45-minute mark.
Add ⅓ oz. Citra hops at the 10-minute mark.
Add 3 oz. of orange zest at the 5-minute mark.
Add ⅓ oz. of cilantro at the 3-minute mark.
Add ⅓ oz. of sage at the 3-minute mark.
Add ½ lb. of cane sugar at the 1-minute mark.

Ferment with Belgian Saison Ale yeast at 72° F until approximately the last three days of the fermentation, then let it rise no higher than 77° F. The real differentiator for a Belgian saison is truly the yeast. The yeast gives it its character.

Note: Le Cygne Noir Saison is bottle conditioned and krausened.

OG 1.053
FG 1.012
ABV 5.4
IBU 19
SRM 31

Wildling Ale

It's no secret Game of Thrones was one of my all time favorites! So I made several beers that were GOT themed. Tyrion Lannister was my favorite character. I've made a beer after him too, similar to this one except it had hibiscus, orange zest and sage added to it with a more fruity estery kviek yeast strain.

8 lbs. of American 2-row Pale malt
1 lb. of Munich malt
1 lb. of Rye malt
Mash at 150° F for 75 minutes.

Kettle Sour.

Inoculate wort with wild things in a boil kettle by opening it up to the air and covering it with cheese cloth for at least a day. I normally don't go over 3 days. This is also to taste; taste the wort to see if it reaches the complexities you're looking for.

Boil for 90 minutes.

Add ⅓ oz. Nugget hops at the 45-minute mark.

Ferment with a clean Kviek yeast at 80° F for initial pitch then let the temperature it rise naturally.

Note: Wildling Ale is bottle conditioned and the Kviek yeast cleans it up nicely.

OG 1.051
FG 1.008
ABV 5.6
IBU 19
SRM 6

My Lunatic Series of Beers.

DAVID SLOCUM

Lunatic Hopped Voodoo Cock Ale

This painting was done by a local artist David Ibarra. Every now and a then you'll run across an artistic genius. Ibarra is one of the most talented artists I've ever seen with his freestyle spray paint murals to his hand drawn beer labels. He has done some of my labels and murals which turned out original and fantastic.

This was the first beer from my Lunatic Series of beers. This was inspired by the famous Cock ale, a 17th- and 18th-century recipe in which you actually throw a parboiled chicken and some spices into the beer after its done fermenting.

I figured, if I call it my Lunatic Series, then it would excuse me for being a lunatic brewer.

10 lbs. of American 2-row pale malt
1.5 lbs. of Munich malt
1 lb. of Victory malt
½ lb. of chocolate malt
½ lb. of brown sugar
4 lbs. of smoked cock bones
Mash at 155° F for 60 minutes.
Sparge and Recirculate.
Boil for 90 minutes.
Add ⅓ oz. Nugget hops at the 60-minute mark.
Add 1 lb. of cock bones at the 60-minute mark.
Add ⅓ oz. Nugget hops at the 45-minute mark.
Add 1 lb. of cock bones at the 45-minute mark.
Add 0.6 oz. Tettnanger hops at the 30-minute mark.
Add 1 lb. of cock bones at the 30-minute mark.

Add 0.6 oz. Tettnanger hops at the 15-minute mark.

Add 1 lb. of spiced cock bones at the 15-minute mark.

Note: I created a spice mix for the mesquite smoked cock bones that has raisins, cloves, and allspice. For the last addition of cock bones, you'll want to use a boil bag to avoid any clogged transfers due to the raisins.

Ferment with California Ale yeast or equivalent at 72° F.

OG 1.066

FG 1.015

ABV 6.6

IBU 40

SRM 14

Mole Madre Ale

This beer was a spinoff of my original Mole Ale. With Mole Madre, I took it a step further and added the smoked chicken bones for a savory smokey flavor. Chicken is normally what mole sauce has in it, so it was natural for me to do this beer.

If you think about Mexican mole, it basically has flavors of mild spiciness, bittersweetness, and chile spice, which comes together harmoniously to create one of the most unique and beautiful tasting things on earth. It's basically an evolving sauce passed down from generation to generation to create perfection.

I wanted to capture at least a little bit of the magnificent tasting flavors of mole into a beer.

8 lbs. of American 2-row pale malt

1 lb. of Munich malt

1 lb. of Victory malt
½ lb. of crystal malt 40L
½ lb. of crystal malt 120L
½ lb. of chocolate malt
2 lbs. of mole
2 lbs. of mesquite smoked cock bones
Mash at 155° F for 60 minutes.
Sparge and Recirculate.
Boil for 90 minutes.
Add ⅓ oz. Nugget hops at the 45-minute mark.
Add 1 lb. of cock bones at the 40-minute mark.
Add 1 lb. of cock bones at the 20-minute mark.
Add 2 lbs. of mole at the 20-minute mark.

Note: This mole is made custom for brewing and is slightly different than we would make to serve as an entree. You can see the recipe under Sauces in Part Four.

Ferment with California Ale yeast or equivalent at 66° F.
OG 1.060
FG 1.014
ABV 6
IBU 14
SRM 27

Three Little Pigs Porter

I'm not the first to ever do this beer. In fact, there is a Mangalista Pig Head Porter that is award-winning. Naturally, it got me curious. This is my version.

8 lbs. of American 2-row pale malt

1 lb. of brown malt
1 lb. of crystal malt 80L
1 lb. of chocolate malt
1 mesquite smoked pig head from a 45 lb. pig or less
Mash at 155° F for 60 minutes.
Sparge and Recirculate.
Boil for 90 minutes.
Add ⅓ oz. Nugget hops at the 45-minute mark.
Add the pig's head at the 20-minute mark.
Note: You'll probably want to put the pig head into a boil bag so that it's easy to take it all out.
Ferment with California Ale yeast or equivalent at 66° F.
OG 1.053
FG 1.013
ABV 5.3
IBU 15
SRM 33

Spicoli Ale

Making this beer was a lot of fun. It took a while for me to get a recipe that I was okay with. Back in them days I was a total goof brewing all kinds of crazy stuff while having a lot of fun doing it I made this beer very early on within a year of being in business. My rational for this beer even though it sounds crazy is that if people like Cheladas and Red Beers then why not a Pizza Beer?

8 lbs. of American 2-row pale malt
1 lb. of crystal malt 60L

1 lb. of Victory
1 large beer thick crust pepperoni pizza
½ tsp of Irish Moss.
Mash at 155° F for 60 minutes.
Add pizza to mash.

I made my own Beer Pizza. You'll want to dry out the pizzas overnight then add it to the start of the mash.

Also do not use lard or any grease, only use flour and beer for the crust. Add roasted squished tomatoes for the pizza sauce then top with pepperonis.

Beer Pizza

Pizza is a lifelong love of mine since childhood. Basically the key to brewing a good pizza is all in the crust whether it's a thin crust or a thick crust. The ingredients on top of the pizza are not so important because you really just put what your taste buds love.

I personally love rustic breads and that's what I go for in my pizza crust.

Note: for Spicoli Ale you are only making a beer crusted pizza with pizza sauce and pepperonis. You'll make the crust with pizza sauce and pepperonis for topping. Add as much pepperonis and pizza sauce as possible.

Ingredients.
3 cups of bread flour
1 pack of active dry yeast
1 tsp of sugar
Half pint of beer (I tend to go for stout of amber ales)

Instructions.

1. Add yeast to warm beer and let sit for at least 15 minutes.
2. Stir in the rest of the ingredients.
3. Form dough into a ball and cover.
4. Let dough rise and sit until the next day when you're ready to make the pizzas.
5. Preheat oven to its highest temp which is normally around the 500 range.
6. Grab a big handful of dough and shape into something that resembles somewhat of a circle.
   If you want it thin then gently press and stretch the pizza dough until you get it to your liking.
   For light fluffy crust you stretch and fold the perimeter of the dough under on the edges to make it light and fluffy or thick if you like. If you want it bready then after you shape your pizza dough, leave the perimeter of the dough in a thick cylinder shape how you like...
7. Let the shaped pizza dough sit for an hour.
8. Baste the crust if you like with egg wash, beer, butter or olive oil. Whatever you like best but for a nice medium browning I recommend eggs and stout beer mix.
   Note: You wouldn't do this for making a pizza for Spicoli, you would skip this step unless you wanted to baste it with beer. I normally use a stout of some kind, like a RIS.
9. Bake for 5 to 10 minutes depending on how thick and big your crust is.

Note: When making the pizza dough, if it's a little too sticky then put a good layer of flour on the surface where you shape the dough and sprinkle some on top of the dough too.

Pizza Sauce.

6 roasted and peeled Roma tomatoes
1 Tsp of black pepper and salt
1 fresh sprig of basil
1 fresh sprig of oregano

Instructions.

1. Put ingredients in a blender with half pint Pale Ale and puree.

Boil for 90 minutes.

Add ⅓ oz. Nugget hops at the 45-minute mark.

Add 1 cup of pepperoni and pizza sauce at the 15 minute mark.

Add ½ teaspoon of Irish Moss at the 15 minute mark.

Ferment with California Ale yeast or equivalent at 66° F.

Note: I've also used Saison yeast strains and had good results. The spice peppery flavor complements the pepperoni.

OG 1.050
FG 1.010
ABV 5.3
IBU 25
SRM 11

10

PART FOUR: EL GUAPO'S KITCHEN

11

Borderland Avant-garde and Fusion Food.

Borderland Avant-garde and Fusion Food.

Sun Brewing Originals – Cooking with beer and my fermented food.

"When a man's stomach is full, it makes no difference whether he is rich or poor."
— Euripides.

Pub Beer Food.

Tripitas Dog.

The Tripitas dog is one of my all-time favorites, ladies and gents! It's a true Sun Brewing original.

This is real gourmet stuff...

Tripitas.

You can prepare the tripitas (beef intestines) yourself or buy them ready to fry.

How to make them from stratch:

1. Rinse and clean thoroughly.
2. Boil the tripe for 30 minutes on a low boil.
3. Cut the tripitas into small chunks, roughly an inch to a few inches.
4. Heat a little lard in a frying pan.
5. Fry the tripitas until crispy on the outside and soft on the inside, roughly 7 to 8 minutes or so. You'll know

when you're close when what I call "the milk" starts to come out while frying.

Tripitas Dog.

1. Boil a jumbo dog in beer for a few minutes or so.
2. Slice the dog lengthwise about ¾ of the way through. You want to split it open but not cut it into two pieces.
3. Grill the dog to sear it a bit on both sides.
4. Place the dog in the hot dog bun, then top with the tripitas.
5. Top the tripitas dog with white onions and cilantro.
6. Serve with a side of salsa.

Note: That is the basics of the tripitas dog, but you can go crazy with these. Try buttering the buns and grilling them. Also, most people like their tripitas crunchy and well done. I personally like them with just enough crunch on the outside while still being a little soft on the inside.

When you boil the tripitas you could also use spices like salt or even boil them in beer.

Suggested Beer Pairing:
Tepache IPA
The Third Edge Vienna Lager

Barbacoa Burger

The beauty of burgers is that you can experiment endlessly with them and find something to please everyone.

This is a very special burger—easily the greatest specialty burger I've ever made. Mexican barbacoa meat is slow cooked for 24 hours, then wrapped in a corn tortilla and deep fried. Have I got your attention?

I serve this burger with delicious homemade sesame seed beer burger buns. Homemade from bun to bun!

There are two basic ways I prepare this burger for serving. The first way leans American with cheese and lettuce; the other way leans Mexican with cilantro, onions, salsa, and lime.

Instructions.

1. Form the barbacoa burger patties and grill them just enough to make a little crust on both sides to somewhat keep the burger formed.
2. Wrap the burger patty in the uncooked corn tortilla and connect the tortilla edges by pressing the masa together so that you completely encapsulate the burger.
3. Deep fry the barbacoa burgers at 350° F for a few minutes or until golden and brown.
4. Assemble the burger with toasted bun and lettuce,

avocado, red onion, jack cheese, salsa, and cilantro. Serve with lime wedge.

Barbacoa.

   5 lbs. chuck roast
   Garlic clove
   1 onion minced
   2 tsp. of cumin
   2 tsp. of oregano
   5 cloves
   1 pint of porter
   3 bay leaves
   Salt and pepper
   Instructions.
Slow cook in crock pot for 8 hours.

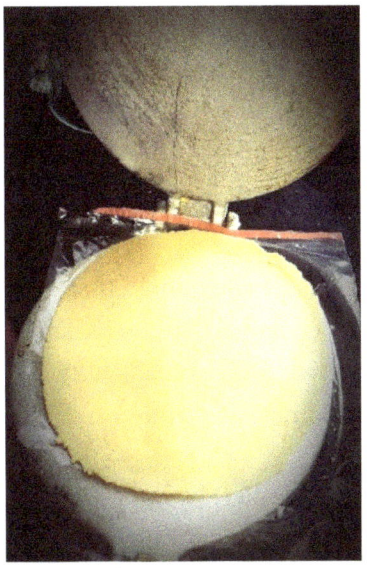

Corn Tortillas.

2 cups masa harina
2 tsp. of lard
1 cup of warm water
1 tsp. of salt

Instructions.

1. Mix ingredients, cover, and let sit for 30 minutes.
2. Grab a small piece of dough and either roll them on a floured area or take two pieces of plastic wrap (one piece for the bottom and one for the top of the press) and put the dough in the tortilla press.
3. Heat up a skillet on medium heat and cook the tortillas a few minutes per side or until desired brownness.

Suggested Beer Pairing:
Left Turn at Albuquerque Pale Ale
Avocado Sour Ale

Brisket Waffle Sandwich

This sandwich had to be done! I first made one on Cooking with El Guapo, and it was so much fun. Who don't like a waffle sandwich? And beer has always been the secret ingredient to a good Belgian waffle.

Instructions.

1. Pull some beer brisket (below) from the oven with a couple of forks.
2. Place brisket in between two Belgian waffles with pickles, cucumbers, and cherry tomatoes.

Beer Brisket.

3 lbs. of beef brisket (rub salt and pepper all over brisket)
1 quart of stout beer

4 oz. of Worcestershire sauce

Add ingredients to crock pot or to foil pan covered with aluminum foil and cook on low for 8 hours.

Belgian Waffles.

2 cups of flour
1 cup of saison beer
½ cup of milk
¼ cup of melted butter
2 eggs
¼ cup of sugar
1 tsp. of salt
1 tsps of baking soda

1. Mix ingredients in a bowl to create a smooth, creamy batter. If it's too thick, add more beer.
2. Butter Belgian waffle iron.
3. Pour Belgian waffle batter into waffle iron and heat until done.

Suggested Beer Pairing:
Frankenstein Hybrid Ale
100% Spontaneous Ale – Charlemagne's Holy Grail

Beer-Battered Frog Legs

Delicious and balanced fried frog legs. They taste like

chicken! No, not really... Frog legs, to me, have a very mild taste, and the seasoning and deep frying adds a layer of texture and taste. This is great to impress someone on a date!

24 oz. Pilsner lager
1 tsp. of garlic salt
1 tsp. of Old Bay
1 lb. of frog legs
1½ cups of flour
1 cup of white corn meal

Instructions.

1. Make the corn beer batter in a bowl by combing the cornmeal, flour, spices, and beer.
2. Heat up deep fryer to 350° F.
3. Dip frog legs into beer corn batter and deep fry for 3 to 5 minutes.
4. Serve with hot sauce or garlic aioli.

Suggested Beer Pairing:
Saison de Membrillo
Nincompoop IPA

Sun Brewing Tacos

2 lbs. chorizo
1 lb. buche
1 lb. bacon strips (thick-cut, smoked pepper bacon)
3 lbs. pork stew meat
1 onion
2 green bell pepper
3 jalapeños
3 chipotles
1 tsp. of salt
1 tsp. of cumin
1 pint of Vienna lager

Instructions.

For this particular discada, there's no order to cooking the ingredients. Throw it all on the disco at the same time.

1. Chop the bacon into squares.
2. Dice the onion and bell pepper. Alternatively, cut them into long strips.
3. Dice the jalapeños and chipotles.
4. Coat the disco (or a griddle) with some lard.
5. Heat up the disco either by gas or wood. I always use wood fire.
6. Put all ingredients in the disco. Add the Vienna lager last and pour it all over the meat.
7. You'll need to stir frequently and monitor closely until finished. It will take at least an hour to cook over wood.
8. Serve in my fried flour tortilla shells with diced white onions, sliced avocados, diced tomatoes, sour cream, and salsa.

Flour Tortillas.

2 cups of flour
1 tsp. of lard
1 tsp. of salt
3 oz. of warm water

Instructions.

1. Mix ingredients in a bowl to form dough.
2. Knead dough into a smooth ball.
3. Cover dough and let rest for an hour.
4. Grab a small handful of dough and roll into a ball.
5. Use a rolling pin if you like. I find using a beer bottle works just fine to roll out the dough.

You'll need to experiment a bit to see what handful you grab is the size you want. It doesn't take much dough to roll out a 5- or 6-inch flour tortilla. I make them about fajita sized.

6. Heat up a cast iron pan, **comal**, skillet, or whatever you're going to use to medium heat.
7. Place flour tortilla in cast iron pan and cook until the dough starts to bubble a bit. Then flip to cook the other side. It takes roughly a minute to a minute and a half.

Note: I'm not using yeast, so time isn't as much as a factor for proofing. Proofing is letting the bread rise because of the yeast activating. We let the tortilla dough rest to allow for the dough to come together from any residual liquids. The dough absorbs the liquids to make a softer mouthfeel for a tortilla.

Fried Tortillas.

1. Fill the frying pan with at least a couple of inches of canola oil and heat on medium.
2. Test the oil by putting a small tortilla dough ball in the heated oil. If it rises to the top quickly, then the oil is ready.
3. Follow the instructions above for the flour tortillas except roll them thicker and longer—in the neighborhood of 7 inches—and you do not need to heat them on a comal. Take the dough straight to be fried.
4. Fold the tortilla into a taco shell and fry half of it at a time. Fry on one side for approximately 30 seconds,

then do the other side. The taco shell should be hard enough to hold its shape.

Note: See below for more of my discada recipes and processes. Also, the Sun Brewing Stout Flour Tortillas (see Beer Breads) go excellent with discadas.
Suggested Beer Pairing:
Canutillo Malt Liquor
Tepache Tamarindo Ale

Discada Tacos.

There is nothing as special as discada for a family gathering! There are a million and one ways to make it, and one is not better than the other. For me, it's a question of what am I in the mood for and what is the setting?

The recipe below is something similar I've had in the neighborhoods with some of my old friends when we want to make a quick and easy discada. The possibilities are endless for combinations; I've used clams in discada before.

1½ lbs. chorizo
1 lb. bacon
1 pack of red hots (hot dogs)
3 lbs. ground beef
1 large onion
2 green bell peppers
3 jalapeños
3 chipotles
1 tsp. of salt and black pepper
1 tsp. of El Guapo Mexican Chile Mix
1 tsp. of cumin
Tall boy of American lager (24oz)

Instructions.

1. Chop up the bacon into squares.
2. Chop up the onion and pepper either by dicing them or cutting into long strips. I tend to use strips.
3. Slice the hot dogs into half inch discs (the short way).
4. Coat the disco, skillet, or griddle with some lard.
5. Heat up the disco either by gas or wood. I always use wood fire.

6. Put all ingredients in the disco but put the tall boy last and pour all over the meat.
7. You'll need to stir frequently and monitor closely until finished. It will take at least 45 minutes to cook.
8. Serve with corn tortillas, guacamole, and salsa.

Beer-nuts Battered Fried Pork Chops

This beer-nut batter is to die for! It adds an extra layer of flavor and texture to the fried chops. Beer nuts taste different depending on the type of beer you get the spent grains from and if you seasoned the spent grains when roasting them. A simple alternative to these fried pork chops is to reduce an amber ale to make a beer glaze and drizzle it over a nice chop while you cook it.

Instructions.

1. Marinate pork chops in amber ale for at least 8 hours.
2. Fill a frying pan with a couple of inches of canola oil and heat on medium heat.

3. Season pork chops to taste. For me, it depends on what mood I'm in. In this case, I'm going for some Old Bay.
4. Dip the seasoned pork chops in the beer batter, then coat them in the flour mixture. Turn each chop in the beer-nuts mixture until it's completely coated.
5. Place in frying pan and turn every few minutes or so until golden and brown.

Note: If you wanted some spice, then marinate in hot sauce. This is a great technique, but use extra-hot sauce. You need to marinate at a hotter level than you actually want to taste because you lose some heat when frying. Many times, I found myself going to great lengths to make Nashville-hot fried chicken when I could have easily marinated overnight in some habanero hot sauce.

Beer Batter.

   2 cups flour
   1 pint of Amber Ale
   1 tsp. of salt
   3 tsp. of Old Bay
   2 eggs
Note: Add more beer if it's too thick and more flour if it's too thin.

Beer Nuts Mixture.

   1 cup flour

1 cup beer nuts
1 tsp. of salt
1 tsp. of brown sugar
3 tsp. of Old Bay
Suggested Beer Pairing:
Old School Love Altbier
Sun Black Ice Lager

3rd Anniversary Rum Raisin Tamales

Sweet Tamales for Brewing Tamale Top Ale

These sweet tamales were made for my 3rd Anniversary Tamale Top Ale as an ingredient for the beer as well as a dish pairing.

Note: You'll need a large pot with a steamer rack for this recipe.

3 cinnamon sticks
1 oz. of anise seed
1 pint Mason jar of golden raisins aged in rum for at least a day

1 pint Mason jar of membrillo slices aged in rum for at least a few hours
Tamale masa (see below)
Tamale Top Ale or amber ale
1 package of corn husks or banana leaves

Instructions.

1. If you are going to use corn husks, soak them in water for 1 hour first.
2. Put cinnamon sticks in the bottom of the tamale pot and fill with water to the false bottom.
3. Invert a pint glass in the middle of the pot. This is to hold the tamales in place and support them as we build circular layers.
4. Tear strings off of the end of the banana leaves or corn husks. This is to tie a bow around the banana leaves to hold your tamales together.
5. Mix the masa in a large bowl (see below).
6. Dump rum-soaked raisins into the masa.
7. Dump just the rum from the membrillo Mason jar into the masa.
8. Pour anise into the masa.
9. Pour 4 oz. of Tamale Top Ale or amber ale into the masa and use your hands to mix it all together. The consistency should be similar to a thick pancake batter. If it's too thick, pour in more beer to thin it out.
10. Scoop the masa into the center of the banana leaves, then place a cube of rum-soaked membrillo in the middle.

11. Fold leaves like a burrito but with one end open: Fold bottom, then left side over, then right side over.
12. Then tie the tamale with the banana strips you tore off to hold the tamale together. Place the tamale in the pot.
13. Repeat this process, layering the tamales in a circular pattern around the inside of the pot, starting against the pot wall for your first layer. Continue to do this until you reach top of the pint glass in the center.
14. If you want to fill the entire pot, then put a plastic bag over the first layer of tamales and repeat the process until the pot is full.
15. Put the lid on the tamale pot and cook on low heat for 2 hours.

Note: If you are using corn husks, the rough edges go on the outside and you scoop the masa onto the smooth edges.

Tamale Masa.

½ cup of lard
½ cup of sugar
2 cups of masa harina
1½ cup of water
Mix all ingredients together.
Suggested Beer Pairing:
Tamale Top Ale
Atole Breakfast Stout

6th Anniversary Chocolate Fig Tamales

See 6th Anniversary Tamale Top Ale for picture.
3 lbs. of masa
30 figs
Stout Beer Ganache (see Sauces)
30 corn husks

Instructions.
Assemble the tamales according to the instructions for 3rd Anniversary Rum Raisin Tamales, using the Sweet Tamale Masa and Stout Ganache-Dipped Figs (recipes below) instead of the membrillo.

Note: If you are using corn husks, the rough edges go on the outside and you scoop the masa on the smooth edges on the inside.

Sweet Tamale Masa.

- 4 cups of masa harina
- ½ cup of shortening
- 1 stick of butter
- 2 cups of sugar
- 9 oz. of evaporated milk.
- 2 tsp. of baking powder
- 1 tsp. of ground cinnamon
- 4 tsp of anise
- 2 cups of ground Abuelita chocolate
- 6 oz. of chopped pecans
- 1 cup of fig jam

1 lb. of purple figs dried and diced
Instructions.

Mix ingredients and knead until combined. If mixture is too thin, then add flour. If the mixture is too thick, then add milk.

Stout Ganache-Dipped Figs.

Prepare Stout Ganache (see Desserts).
Dip figs in stout ganache and put in the fridge for at least an hour to solidify.
Suggested Beer Pairing:
100% Spontaneous - 6th Anniversary Tamale Top Ale
Nirvana Russian Kvas

My Fermented Food.

The Fermented Sope.

The idea of this came from the yeast starter for my spontaneous fermented breads. I make it with fermented bread tortillas and fermented toppings.

The essence of this sope is the fermented tortilla and the fermented ingredients. You don't have to use kimchi; you could use non-spiced, fermented cabbage, instead. The idea is to have a sour and spice flavor from fermentation. For a little crunch, you could sprinkle some Beer Nuts Cereal on top (see Soups).

Yeast starter tortillas (see below)
Spanish chorizo
Kimchi
Pickled peppers.
Stinky cheese (cotija)
Mexican crème
Fermented hot sauce

Yeast Starter Tortillas

1. Make wild yeast starter by taking 4 oz. of green 100% spontaneous ale or any 4 oz. of unfinished ale. Take

this warm, live ale and add 4 oz. of flour and let sit for at least 48 hours. The longer the fermentation the better. The ideal length for yeast starter fermentation is 1 week.

Note: You'll know the starter is ready when there are a lot of bubblies and it increases in size. Use a 50/50 ratio of beer to flour.

2. Once the yeast starter is finished to desired consistency, pour it straight to the frying pan with an inch of canola oil. You could also pre-shape the fermented bread to make Fried Sope Tortillas. Or add some spice even beer nuts (see Soups) to them while preshaping.
3. Assemble sope with chorizo, kimchi, peppers, cotija cheese, crème, and hot sauce.

Instructions for Frying Sope Tortillas.

1. Mix ingredients in a bowl to form dough.
2. Form dough into a smooth ball.
3. Cover dough and let rest for an hour.
4. Grab a small handful of dough and roll it out. Use a rolling pin if you like. I find using a beer bottle works just fine to roll out the dough. Roll it out thick enough to sustain frying. You can fold up the edges a bit like a pizza crust if you like.
5. Fill the frying pan with at least a couple of inches of canola oil and heat on medium.
6. Test the oil by putting a small tortilla dough ball in

the heated oil. If it rises to the top quickly, then the oil is ready.
7. Lightly fry, just until beginning to turn brown at the edges.

Suggested Beer Pairing:
Saison de Membrillo
Gypsy Dude IPA

Fermented Beer Batter-Fried Chicken.

The idea came from watching the beginning of the yeast starter ferment from sourdough bread. It starts to get bubbly but not too doughy, yet. I thought, "Lets dip some chicken in it and fry it!"

You can see the texture is different from fermented beer batter. I also added beer-nuts to the top of the chicken before frying.

Yeast starter for the beer batter (see Fermented Sope for yeast-starter)

Beer nuts (see Soups)
Chicken

Instructions.

1. Parboil chicken in beer so that the chicken is mostly cooked.
2. In a cast iron pan, preheat a couple of inches of canola oil to medium heat.
3. Dip the chicken into the yeast starter until it's completely coated.
4. Sprinkle beer nuts over the top of the battered chicken.
5. Fry until golden and a brown on both sides.

Suggested Beer Pairing:
Symposius Sour Porter
The Third Edge Vienna Lager

Fermented Chamoy Eggs.

I absolutely love this concept: pickled green chamoy hard-boiled eggs paired with my Green Chamoy Pickle Sour Lager! This is a versatile dish. You could do a lot with it, like make it into a dessert by adding some cream or fruits like apricots or add it to a salad for a meal. A nice snack would be to add it to some toast with avocado slices, or add diced ham on top to have chamoy eggs and ham.

SUN BREWING COMPANY COOKBOOK SECOND EDITION

Instructions.

1. Place a single layer of eggs at the bottom of a saucepan and cover with water approximately a couple of inches above the eggs.
2. Bring water to roiling boil, then turn to low heat and cover saucepan.
3. Strain eggs after 15 minutes while running water over the eggs to cool them off.
4. Peal eggs and place into a container with salt brine of at least 10 percent solution. A typical 10 percent solution is 10 grams of salt per 100 ml of water. That's approximately a pint of salt for a gallon of water.
5. We'll use 2 quarts of water and 1 cup of Kosher salt for saltwater solution.
6. Add a pint of green chamoy sauce to the salt brine.
7. Let ferment for at least a few days but a good week is what I recommend.
8. Cut eggs in half like deviled eggs and sprinkle paparika or whatever kind of pepper you like. Tajin is another

great choice. If you wanted to add more than spice, try sliced avocados.

Note: See Pickling section below for more information on pickling. Also, you can use a starter if you like with a pint of tepache (see Beverages). Use a starter if you want a quicker fermentation of a few days.
Suggested Beer Pairing:
You Don't Know Jack! Fruit IPA
Green Chamoy Pickle Sour Lager

Sun Brewing's Hot Sauce.

I like to put this hot sauce in a bowl with olives.

1 lb. of New Mexican red chile peppers or any red chile peppers to ferment
1 cup of Tepache Vinegar (see Sauces) or apple cider vinegar
1 quart of purified water
2 tsp. of salt

Fermenting Peppers.

1. Wash peppers.
2. Cut stems off.
3. Dice them up or mix in a blender.
4. Add to mixing bowl.
5. Add at least 1 tsp. of salt per 12 oz.
6. Put in a Mason jar and punch down to pack them real good and remove air pockets.
7. Pour purified water into mason jar, leaving 1 inch of headspace, then screw on lid.
8. Leave at room temperature away from light and ferment for at least two weeks. The longer you ferment, the better the taste.

Finishing the Hot Sauce.

9. Pour Mason jar into blender and blend it to hot sauce consistency.
10. Pour blended sauce into a saucepan and add Tepache Vinegar.
11. Bring to a boil for 5 minutes then put on low heat to simmer for 10 minutes.
12. Pour hot sauce straight from the boil into sanitized sauce bottles, then cap.

Note: You need to sanitize all equipment just like you would for brewing. If there is mold, then throw away the fermented chiles and start over.

Note for green hot sauce: Use Big Jim (Hatch green chile

peppers) and serranos. Cilantro is another nice addition. If you do not have access to Hatch green chiles, then use common green chiles like poblanos.

Suggested Beer Pairing:
Nicodemus Ale or a fruit ale
Nincompoop IPA

100% Spontaneous Fermented Bread.

My 100% spontaneous fermented breads could be viewed as variants of sourdough. The key difference is that traditional sourdough is made from a yeast starter. My 100% spontaneous fermented bread differs from sourdough in that my yeast starter is made from 100% Spontaneous Ale and the spontaneous fermented bread is made from flour and spontaneous ale. Sometimes, I do not use a starter for these breads because I use live 100% Spontaneous Ale mixed in with the flour, which ferments the dough over days.

1 pint of warm live 100% Spontaneous Ale

Note: If you do not have spontaneous ale, then use a pale ale. Most of the wild yeast comes from the flour. However, the wild yeast from the spontaneous ale truly makes this bread over the top.

3 cups of bread flour

1 tsp. of sea salt

Instructions without yeast starter.

1. Mix all the ingredients together and squish and mix well with your hands.
2. Fold the dough and punch it down until it starts becoming smooth.
3. Shape dough into ball shape, cover with a towel, and keep at room temperature.
4. Keep kneading every 3 to 6 hours for the next 24 hours.

5. Let rest for at least 24 hours or until it increases in size at room temperature. Let it sit for longer than 24 hours if you have to... the dough will be ready when it's approximately doubled in size, but it doesn't have to rise that much because it could be a weaker fermentation.
6. Grease a Dutch oven.
7. Bake in Dutch oven at 450° F for 30 minutes, covered. Then uncover until browned to your liking. If you want the bread dark, then be sure to have a water pan of boiling water in the oven and have the Dutch oven uncovered.

Instructions with yeast starter.

1. Make wild yeast starter by taking 4 oz. of green 100% spontaneous ale or any 4 oz. of unfinished ale. Take this warm, live ale and add 4 oz. of flour and let sit for at least 48 hours. The longer the fermentation, the better. The ideal length for yeast starter fermentation is 1 week. You'll know the starter is ready when there are a lot of bubblies and it increases in size.
Note: This 4 oz. should come from your pint of ale from the ingredients.
2. Put a pan of water in the oven and preheat it to its highest setting (at least 450°). It should be nice and steaming by the time you put the dough in.
3. Mix all the ingredients together and knead with your hands until smooth and elastic.

4. Shape dough into ball, cover with a towel, and keep at room temperature overnight.
5. When the dough has risen, score the dough and immediately start baking it.
6. Bake in oven until browned to your liking. If you want the bread darker and glossier, then be sure to have a water pan of steaming water in the oven at the beginning of the baking. If you wanted, you could take out the water pan after 15 minutes but it's not necessary.

Note: You could make a lot of different flour combinations with different ingredients. You could add spices that you like, as well. For the picture above, I used beer nuts with the recipe. Keep reading for a jazzed up spontaneous fermented bread.

Suggested Beer Pairing:
Avocado Sour Ale
100% Spontaneous Ale - Tepache Ale

100% Spontaneous Fermented Bread made with Ale, Jalapeños, and Stout Ganache.

1 pint of warm 100% Spontaneous Ale
2 cups of bread flour
1 cup of Hungarian wheat flour
1 tsp. of salt
3 diced red jalapenos
2 oz. of Stout Beer Ganache (see Sauces)

Note: If you do not have 100% spontaneous beer, then use regular beer. The wild yeast mostly comes from the flour. Using spontaneous ales gives it an unmatched complexity and flavor while also adding to the fermentation process.

If you don't have stout ganache, then use chocolate syrup and beer mixed together. Mix just a little beer and add chocolate bark so that it stays thick.

Instructions.

1. Make wild yeast starter by taking 4 oz. of green 100% spontaneous ale or any 4 oz. of unfinished ale. Take this warm, live ale and add 4 oz. of flour and let sit for at least 48 hours. The longer the fermentation, the better. The ideal length for yeast starter fermentation is 1 week. You'll know the starter is ready when there are a lot of bubbles and it increases in size.
   Note: This 4 oz. should come from your pint of ale from the ingredients.
2. Mix all the ingredients together and squish with your hands until mixed well and rustic looking.
3. Shape dough into ball shapes and cover with plastic wrap.
4. Let rest at room temperature or a little on the warm

side, approximately 70° F for at least 12 to 24 hours or until doubled in size. If you need to let sit for longer than 24 hours, that's okay... the dough will be ready when it's approximately doubled in size.
5. Grease a Dutch oven.
6. Bake in Dutch oven at 450° F for 30 minutes covered. Then uncover until browned to your liking. If you want the bread dark, it usually takes another 30 minutes.

Suggested Beer Pairing:
Le Cygne Noir Black Saison
100% Spontaneous IPA – Beyond the Pale

Preservation.

Understanding the pH value of foods.

All food is either high acid or low acid depending on the pH value. When Mason jarring, all recipes must be at least 4.6 pH or lower.

There are several ways to achieve a 4.6 pH value or to lower the ph value. For example, if you want to preserve a low-acid food, then you could combine it with a high-acid food to bring the pH level down. You would need a pH tester to ensure you have the right pH value or you risk the food spoiling.

Examples of high-acid foods are lemons, pickles, peaches, and apricots.

Examples of low-acid foods are carrots, beans, and okra.

Important: Low-acid foods such as vegetables and meats

should be pressurized and canned. Pressurizing and canning is beyond the scope of this book. However, you could always buy a pressurized canner. You would follow the same principles in this book, but it would require special equipment.

If you choose to use the boiling water method for Mason jarring low-acid foods that have borderline pH values, like carrots, then recognize you're not going to have a long shelf life. You could always squirt some lime juice into the brine to lower the recipe's pH value, but at the end of the day, carrots are a low-acid food that would need to be pressurized.

Boiling water method.

1. Put filled, capped Mason jars in a stock pot with at least 1 inch of water in the bottom.
2. Put lid on stock pot.
3. Bring to a rolling boil of at least 220° F for at least 15 minutes for pint Mason jars. For quart Mason jars, it would be at least 20 minutes.

Mason Jarring.

Frankenstein Grape Jelly.

I've always loved to simply have a piece of toast. There is something elegant about just sitting with a loved one over a piece of toast and jelly. In this case, it's Frankenstein beer jelly and it's good.

3 cups grapes

2 cups sugar

2 pints of Frankenstein Hybrid Ale (or a beer-wine hybrid ale or fruit beer)

Instructions.

1. Wash grapes and take of the stems.
2. Put ingredients in a saucepan filled with beer.
3. Bring to a boil on medium heat, stirring occasionally until it reaches the gelling point of 220° F, then simmer for 5 minutes.
4. Fill sanitized Mason jar, leaving ½ inch of headspace, then cap.
5. Place jar in stock pot with 1 inch of simmering water.
6. Heat stock pot to medium and bring to a rolling boil for 15 minutes.
7. Turn off heat and let jars cool for 5 minutes.
8. Remove jars from stock pot and let cool for a day.

Suggested Beer Pairing:
Frankenstein Hybrid Ale

Meados de Alien Ale

Note: I tend to put the jelly on my toast, consequently, that's how I paired it.

Mezcal Ancho Chile Guava Marmalade.

5 cups guava
½ lb. of charred ancho chiles soaked in mezcal
6 cups of sugar
3 tsp. of pectin
1 cup Tepache Vinegar (see Sauces) or apple cider vinegar
½ cup of water
Instructions.

1. Finely chop guavas, including skins, and chiles.
2. Dump ingredients into a saucepan. Include the mezcal from the chiles but leave out the pectin for now.
3. Bring to a boil while stirring on high heat, then add pectin.
4. Boil for a few more minutes while stirring or until desired thickness.
5. Fill sanitized Mason jar leaving ¼ inch of headspace, then cap.
6. Place jar in stock pot with 1 inch of simmering water.
7. Heat stock pot to medium and bring to a rolling boil for 15 minutes.
8. Turn off heat and let jars cool for 5 minutes.
9. Remove jars from stock pot and let cool for a day.

Suggested Beer Pairing:
Three Little Pigs Porter
Vagabundo Ale

Note: I tend to put the marmalade on my toast, consequently, that's how I paired it.

Pickling.

Tepache Jalapeño Pickles.

Fermenting food is essentially brining over a few weeks' time. A fermentation brine is 1 cup salt to 2 quarts of water. The key to a good fermentation is maintaining a strong brine strength, at least 10 percent at room temperature (approximately 70° F). I normally go a lot higher than 10 percent.

Cucumbers are a low-acid vegetable, and if you Mason jar to make pickles, they won't have a long shelf life, but they will last longer than in a container in the fridge. I wouldn't leave it sealed in the mason jar for more than a month. If you can pressurize and can the pickles, then your shelf life will last approximately 6 months.

Note: You'll know if something went wrong in your jarring if there are bubbles in your jar.

After fermentation is complete you can cook with them or eat them. They'll last approximately a week in the refrigerator.

1 lb. of sliced cucumbers
½ lb. of jalapeño peppers
2 quarts water
1 cup of salt (preferably pickling salt)
1 quart of Tepache Vinegar (see Sauces) or apple cider vinegar

Fermentation.

Note: Cucumbers have to be submerged under brine for entire fermentation.

1. Combine 1 cup pickling salt and 2 quarts water in a sanitized container.
2. Add cucumbers to brine.
3. Place a plate or object that is slightly smaller than the

fermentation container on top of the cucumbers and jalapenos to keep them submerged.
4. Place some kind of a weight over the plate to ensure cucumbers and jalapenos stay submerged. You could add a sanitized mason jar filled with water or a plastic bag filled with brine.
5. Add ½ cup of salt to brine on the second day of fermentation.
   Note: My general rule is one pint of salt per gallon of water.
6. At the end of 1 week of fermentation add 1 oz. of salt. You should be able to see the bubblies of fermentation at this point.
7. Add 1 oz. of salt every week until 4 weeks or finished fermentation. Scrape off fermentation residue at least once a week. You can scrape off using a sanitized spoon.
8. Fermentation is complete when there are no more bubbles.

Note: Check daily for mold. If there is white or blue mold, then remove it. If it's any color but white or blue, then discard the batch. Mason jar when fermentation is complete or pickled to taste.

Mason Jarring Instructions.

1. Combine 2 quarts of water, 1 cup of salt, and cucumbers and let refrigerate for approximately 8 hours.

2. Combine 2 cups of water and 2 cups of Tepache Vinegar in a saucepan and bring to a boil.
3. Drain cucumbers and jalapeños and add to boil for 3 minutes.
4. Fill sanitized jar, leaving ½-inch headspace.
5. Place jar in stock pot with 1 inch of simmering water.
6. Heat stock pot to medium and bring to a rolling boil for 15 minutes.
7. Turn off heat and let jars cool for 5 minutes.
8. Remove jars from stock pot and let cool for a day.

Suggested Beer Pairing:
Tepache Sour Ale
100% Spontaneous IPA – Beyond the Pale

Chile Red Cabbage.

This could be considered a thick, red, spiced sauerkraut.

1 red cabbage

2 oz. of jalapeños
2 oz. of sea salt
1 tsp. of El Guapo Chile Mix (you can buy this at a Mexican grocery store in the spice section or order online.)
1 tsp. of black pepper
Instructions.

1. Shred cabbage.
2. Slice jalapeños the long way.
3. Combine chile, salt, pepper, jalapeno strips, and cabbage into bowl and mix.
4. Add to brine (2 quarts of water and 1 cup of pickling salt).
5. Place a plate or object that is slightly smaller than the fermentation container on top of the cabbage and jalapeños to keep them submerged.
6. Place a weight over the plate to ensure the cabbage stays submerged.
7. Add ½ cup of salt to brine on the second day of fermentation.
8. Ferment at room temperature, approximately 66° F. At the end of one week of fermentation you should be able to see the bubblies of fermentation. Check for mold at least every other day and remove it with sanitized spoon.
9. Ferment for approximately a month. Fermentation is complete when there are no more bubbles.
10. Put sauerkraut and brine mixture into a pot on low

heat until it reaches 200° F, then mason jar it with ½ inch of head space.

Note: Sauerkraut was meant to be pressurized and packaged. The boiling water method for mason jarring only applies to high-acid foods, consequently if you choose to mason jar using the boiling water method, then the shelf life will not be as long. Two weeks storage should be good; I wouldn't go longer than a month. If you see bubbles in the jar, then something has gone wrong and discard.

Note: Another great idea would be to grill the sauerkraut to get it a little charred then pickle it.

Suggested Beer Pairing:
Narama Ancho Chile Sour Ale
You Don't Know Jack! Fruit IPA

Pickled Grilled Carrots.

Grilled whole carrots
Grilled whole parsnips
Tepache Vinegar (see Sauces)
1 tsp. of salt

Carrot Fermentation.

Fermenting is essentially brining over a few weeks' time. A fermentation brine is 1 cup salt to 2 quarts of water. The key to a good fermentation is maintaining a strong brine strength of at least 10 percent at room temperature, approximately 70° F.

Carrots are a low-acid vegetable, and if you mason jar it then it won't have a long shelf life, but it will last longer than putting them in a container in the fridge. I wouldn't leave it sealed in the mason jar for more than a month. If you can pressurize and can the carrots, then your shelf life will last approximately 6 months.

You'll know if something went wrong if there are bubbles in your jar.

After fermentation is complete, you can cook with them or eat them. They'll last a week in the refrigerator.

1 lb. of grilled whole carrots
2 quarts water
1 cup of salt (preferably pickling salt)
1 quart of vinegar
1 tsp. of turmeric
1 tsp. of mustard seed

Fermentation.

Note: Carrots have to be submerged under brine for the entire fermentation.

1. Combine 1 cup pickling salt and 2 quarts water in a sanitized container.
2. Add grilled carrots to brine.
3. Place a plate or object that is slightly smaller than the fermentation container on top of the carrots to keep them submerged.
4. Place a weight on the plate to ensure the carrots stay submerged.
5. Add ½ cup of salt to brine on the second day of fermentation.
6. At the end of one week of fermentation, add 1 oz. of salt. You should be able to see the bubblies of fermentation at this point.
7. Add 1 oz. of salt every week until 4 weeks or fermentation finishes. Scrape off fermentation residue at least once a week with a sanitized spoon.

Fermentation is complete when there are no more bubbles.

Note: Mason jar when fermentation is complete or pickled to taste.

Mason Jarring Instructions.

1. Combine 2 quarts of water, 1 cup of salt, and cucumbers and let refrigerate for approximately 8 hours.
2. Combine 2 cups of water and 2 cups of Tepache Vinegar in a saucepan and bring to a boil.
3. Drain cucumbers and jalapeños and add to boil for 3 minutes.

4. Fill sanitized jar, leaving ½-inch headspace.
5. Fill a stock pot with 1 inch of water and bring to a simmer.
6. Place jar in stock pot.
7. Heat stock pot to medium and bring to a rolling boil for 15 minutes.
8. Turn off heat and let jars cool for 5 minutes.
9. Remove jars from stock pot and let cool for a day.

Note: You'll probably need to use the small carrots whole or cut the big carrots. I like to use the entire carrot.
Suggested Beer Pairing:
Swords & Ale (or wild or sour ale)
Falkor Belgian Amber Ale

Quick Pickling.

Quick pickling is common in Southwestern Texas, especially in El Paso. A perfect example is chile toreados. Nowadays, chile toreados are made with soy sauce, and I would be willing to bet the Chinese immigrants to Mexico started this tradition. It's very flavorful with soy sauce, and I'll follow this basic recipe for cucumbers also. I'll even sprinkle a little chile on the cucumbers. Delicious!

Chile Toreados.

Roasted chile peppers (usually 4 to 6 jalapeños)
½ small white onion, sliced
1 tsp. of soy sauce

2 tsp. of vinegar (I prefer red wine vinegar or my Tepache Vinegar [see Sauces])
1 lime

Instructions.

1. You can grill the onions and jalapeños if you like, or you could fry the jalapeños. There are several ways to roast chiles. I like to slice the jalapeños or at least press down on them to open them up and let all the juices infuse.
2. Put all the ingredients into a container and refrigerate overnight. Use 1 part soy sauce and 2 parts vinegar.

Suggested Beer Pairing:
Tepache IPA
Falkor Belgian Amber

Generic Quick Pickling Recipe.

This is a great trick if you want to do a pickling to get grilled fruits or grilled vegetables ready for the next day.
1 cup vinegar
1 tsp. of mustard seeds
1 tsp. of salt
Spice of choice
Vegetable of choice

Note: It wouldn't hurt to add beer or liquor to the brine. Also, if you wanted a sweet and sour taste, then add ½ cup of sugar. You could also add soy sauce, which I tend to do a lot.

Instructions.

1. Make the brine.
2. Grill the vegetables to charred.
3. Put vegetables in brine.
4. Refrigerate for at least 3 hours.
5. Serve.

My Borderland Backyard-Style Barbecue.

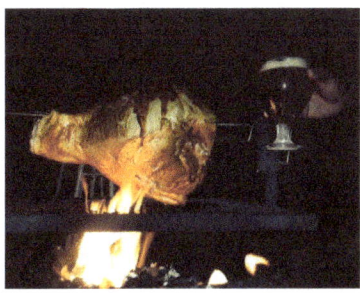

Barbecue is something close to my heart and has been done since the dawn of mankind. To me, barbecue is simply cooking over wood fire slowly. I think every culture has some version of this. Asian barbecue is some of my favorite, whether it's Korean short ribs, Japanese Yakitori, or Chinese Duck. Here in America, we have cultures and subcultures of barbecue. In the South, pork barbecue is king, but here in Texas it's all about the beef. Not one is better than the other, but it's just a stylistic thang. I think there is something to be learned from all the styles of barbecue and to realize that you don't know everything. It's not about being better than somebody else or passing judgement. Barbecue is all about shaping your style from your local environment with your friends and family.

Barbecue, for me, is one of the absolute best ways to celebrate with your family and friends, especially with your beer.

I usually make something outdoors on some kind of concoction barbecue pit—it gets the job done. This BBQ setup a modern art masterpiece.

Barbecue Basics.

Using a Chimney to Start a Fire.

Using a chimney is always best practice because it eliminates using lighter fluid or any flammable liquids to start the fire.

Instructions.

1. Fill the bottom of the chimney with newspaper. Cardboard will work, too.
2. Fill the top with charcoal.
3. Light the newspaper.

4. Let the coals start to glow and then cover over with white ash. This takes approximately 15 minutes.
5. Pour them onto the grill, then add more coals or wood.

Temperature Control.

If the fire starts to flame up from grease or the temperature simply needs to be lowered, then have squirt bottle or squirt gun filled with water to squirt it on the coals to lower the heat. This also adds steam to the cooking which aids in making food tender.

Also, always have a thermometer to at least track ambient heat. There are thermometers to track internal temperatures as well.

Building a grill.

In its simplest form, all you really need is a grate and a couple of cinder blocks. I do this all the time. You could even use a couple of big rocks. In my backyard, I'll grab my wok and place it between two cinder blocks with a fire underneath. You can do a lot with a disc for cooking. If you want a grate, then adjust the blocks the length of your grate and you have a grill. If you want an oven put a large cast iron pot or an outdoor griddle and cover it with your wok or a grill top.

Building a Barbecue Pit and Outdoor Oven.

Building an outdoor oven is the conventional way to roast a whole animal.

1. Purchase foot-long cement blocks, approximately 50.
2. Build a perimeter of foot-long cement blocks at least 4 blocks wide and 8 blocks long.
   The perimeter is good to pile glowing embers and a work area.
3. You'll need to build a goat bed to lay the animal on to slow barbecue. You can get creative with this. You can use cement blocks and chicken wire, or you can lay the blocks two-high in parallel. You can lay the blocks the tall or short way—the main point is to align the animal towards the middle of your cement oven. You can make your barbecue bed higher to keep the goat farther away from the heat, but I wouldn't go lower.
4. On one end of the perimeter, stack cement blocks 4 blocks high and 4–5 blocks long. This setup will do for

a 75 lb. animal or less. Adjust length and width to your goat or pig.

5.

The oven should open into the inside of the barbecue pit. Leave some small openings on each side of the front of the oven to allow for shoveling embers along the perimeter of the oven walls. I simply build three walls of the oven and then use a single stack of cement blocks in the opening.

6. Make a top for the oven with a piece of plywood or any untreated wood. Just cut it to your oven's specifications. You could also use stainless steel transmission oil pans that you can order at an auto parts store; you'll need to order at least two of them.

7. Finally, you will need something to close off the front of the oven such as more cement blocks or planks of wood. Just place the wood over the openings and use a cement block pressed against it to hold it in place.

Fuel Source.

For myself I'll never use a gas or electric grill. I'll only use some kind of charcoal, briquettes, or wood.

Disposing of ash.

Be very careful when you do this. A lot of times you think there are no live embers in the ash when there really is. I recommend always dumping the ashes into some kind of metal bucket or aluminum trash can.

12

Borderland Barbecue Recipes.

Borderland Barbecue Recipes

Pipian Short Ribs.

Pipian is a green mole sauce made with pumpkin seeds. It's an amazing sauce made from fresh ingredients that has a balanced beer-nutty, herbal, and spicy taste.

Green Mole sauce (see Sauces)
Pumpkin seeds
Short ribs

Instructions.

1. Marinate short ribs in stout beer overnight.
2. Heat up wood or charcoals on medium heat until low, glowing embers.
3. Put the short ribs on direct heat and flip in approximately 7 minutes.
4. Cook for approximately 15 minutes until browned.
5. Braise the ribs with pipian sauce if you like, but I spread it over the ribs when I'm finished grilling it. Then sprinkle pumpkin seeds over the dish.

Suggested Beer Pairing:
Symposius Sour Porter
Wasshoppening Wild Malt Liquor

Chamoy Wings.

Chamoy wings are the best wings I've ever made! I loved it so much, I made a whole Cooking with El Guapo episode on how to make them. I'm incredibly surprised nobody has picked up on this yet. I've been doing it for years, and I've yet to see an establishment make them. It's got to pick up, eventually, because it's crazy insane delicious!

Chicken wings and drumsticks
Chamoy sauce (see Sauces)
Instructions.

1. Marinate chicken in beer and salt overnight.
2. Fire up the briquettes. I prefer briquettes, mostly. I get it cost effective and I think it adds more flavor than regular charcoal.
3. Once the briquettes start to ash on medium heat, then add to the grill and flip occasionally.
4. Grill for approximately 30 minutes.
5. Then pull from the grill and put in a bowl with chamoy sauce and mix.

Note: There are a million and one ways to make chamoy wings. You could deep fry them or coat the wings on the grill like a BBQ sauce.

Suggested Beer Pairing:
Chamoy Ale

Left Turn at Albuquerque Pale Ale
Sour ale or fruited pale ale

Stout Beer-Battered Wings.

The stout beer batter gives the batter a deepness of color and flavor to complement savory wings.

Instructions.

1. Fire up grill with briquettes.
2. Grill chicken wings on medium heat for approximately 20 to 25 minutes.
3. Take wings and dip them in stout beer batter and dip

immediately in deep fryer for 3 to 5 minutes or until browned on medium heat.

Stout Beer Batter.

  2 cups flour
  1 pint of stout
  1 tsp. of salt
  3 tsp. of Old Bay
  2 eggs
  Suggested Beer Pairing:
  Cheeky Devil Tropical Stout
  100% Spontaneous Ale - Illegitame non Carborundum Ale

Tamarindo Chicken.

I remember taking this picture when I first opened my brewpub. It brings back good memories experimenting with new flavors. This specific tamarindo chicken was sprinkled with **flechazo** stick sprinklies.

Instructions.

1. Marinate chicken in beer and salt overnight.
2. Fire up the grill with briquettes on one side and put foil pan with beer on the other.
3. Once briquettes reach temperature of approximately 250° F, add a couple chunks of wood for smoking.
4. Season the chicken with salt and pepper and place on indirect heat over the beer foil pan.
5. Brush tamarindo sauce over the chicken over the last 30 minutes of cooking then sprinkle flechazo stick sprinkles over the chicken in the last 5 minutes to let it caramelize.
6. Cook for at least two and a half hours.

Suggested Beer Pairing:
Tamarindo Ale
The Third Edge Vienna Lager

Tomahawk Steak.

How to grill a steak the way I love it! Reverse searing is basically cooking on low heat first then searing it. In this case indirect heat then searing it at the end. The impressive presentation of a tomahawk steak is for special occasions when you really want to impress someone.

Instructions.

1. Sprinkle salt and pepper generously (or your steak rub) and evenly on both sides of steak and refrigerate overnight. I tend to put salt and pepper on generously because of how thick the tomahawks are.
2. Fire up the grill with briquettes on one side of grill and leave the other side empty for indirect heat to cook the steak on.
3. Cook approximately 10 minutes per side total time for medium rare which is the way I love it.
4. At approximately 7 minutes put over high heat then flame it up to sear approximately 1 minute per side or until you get a nice crust.
5. 125 degrees for rare. Use 10 degree increments from rare to well done.

Note: Another great idea is to add a foil pan filled with beer and mesquite wood chips to give a touch of smoke flavor.

Texas Beer Brisket.

Instructions.

1. Trim the fat, if you like, to approximately half an inch. This is optional; I personally do not trim the fat off.
2. Sprinkle salt and pepper generously and evenly all over the brisket and marinate in stout beer overnight. Then freeze the brisket.
   Note: I tend to put a lot of salt and pepper because of how thick briskets are.
3. Fire up the grill with briquettes on one side and a foil pan filled with beer and mesquite wood chunks on the other.
4. Pull brisket out of fridge and let sit for an hour before barbecuing.
5. Once the briquettes are glowing embers, then put several mesquite and cherry wood chunks over the embers.
6. Put brisket, fat-side up, on the indirect heat side of the grill and over the beer foil pan. I personally don't think it's terribly significant to put the fat layer up, but the

idea of it is for the fat to melt on top of the brisket to provide another layer of flavor.

7. Cook approximately 30 minutes per pound at 225° F ambient temperature on indirect heat for rare brisket. Use 5-minute increments from rare to well done at 225° F ambient heat. For example, a medium-done brisket would be 40 minutes per pound at 225° F.
  Note: Because it will be frozen or partially frozen, it will vary in total time cooked. Freezing brisket after seasoning and marinating makes the brisket more succulent.
8. I never wrap my brisket. I love the deep bark flavor to any smoked food. You run the chance of having a drier meat, but from my experience it's not a big chance and you can always put some wet BBQ sauce on it.
9. Let the brisket rest for an hour then slice it down the middle and continue slicing it until all sliced up. A lot of people like real thin slices. As for myself, it's all good.

Suggested Beer Pairing:
Green Chamoy Pickle Ale
Sun Arkhangelisk Russian Imperial Stout

Thanksgiving Beer-Injected Turkey and Granny's Stuffing.

A beer-injected turkey will be the juiciest and most succulent, savory turkey you've ever tasted! It's a must try! This turkey right here is basically a beer-and-butter turkey.
Instructions.

1. Rub salted butter all over the thawed-out turkey.
2. Sprinkle salt and pepper evenly all over turkey and refrigerate overnight. Cover with plastic wrap.
3. Fire up the grill with briquettes on one side and a foil pan filled with beer and applewood chunks on the other.
4. Pull turkey out of the fridge and inject it with beer every few inches or so.
5. Stuff the cavity of the turkey with Granny's Thanksgiving Stuffing (see below).
6. Once the briquettes are glowing embers, place one small applewood chunk in the middle of the embers.
7. Put turkey over the beer-filled foil pan.
8. Barbecue on indirect heat at approximately 300 to 325° F. A 10 lb. turkey takes approximately 3 hours and a 20 lb. turkey takes approximately 4 hours. Use a thermometer to check internal temperature. The turkey is done when the breast registers 170° F.
9. Take the turkey out and let it rest for 30 minutes before serving.

Suggested Beer Pairing:
The Working Man Ice Ale
Tepache Sour Ale

Granny's Thanksgiving Stuffing.

This stuffing is a generational recipe that goes back generations from my Grandma Slocum.

Granny's Southern White Cornbread (see below)

6 celery stalks, diced
1 onion, diced
3 tsp. of sage
2 loaves of dried Wonder bread
Salt and pepper
6 eggs
1 cup of giblet stock
Chopped giblets

Instructions.

1. Make Granny's Southern White Cornbread and let sit overnight to dry out.
2. Use two loaves of white bread and let sit out overnight to dry out.
3. Chop up cooked giblets from giblet stock.

4. Take all ingredients and mix together with your hands, breaking up the cornbread and white bread as you mix all the ingredients. Add more giblet stock as needed to reach a consistency that is not too chunky.
5. Add cooked turkey neck from giblet stock to center of stuffing.
6. Preheat oven to 350° F and bake stuffing for 30 minutes covered with foil, then remove foil and bake for another 30 minutes or until golden and a brown.

Giblet Stock.

1. Sautee giblets and turkey neck in saucepan with butter and canola oil for approximately 5 minutes.
2. Add 3 pints of water with salt, pepper, and sage.
3. Bring to a boil for 3 minutes, then put on low heat to simmer for 2 hours.

Giblet Gravy.

1. Put 1 pint of giblet stock in frying pan on medium heat.
2. Sprinkle in flour while stirring until you reach the thickness desired for your gravy. It's usually 1 or 2 tsps.
3. Add salt, pepper, and sage to taste.
4. Add chopped giblets if you like. I normally save all the giblets for the stuffing, but some people don't like giblets in their stuffing. Consequently, I'll end up making Granny's Stuffing both with giblets and without giblets, but it always has a turkey neck in the middle.

Note: You could also smoke the stuffing or beer-steam the giblet gravy!

Granny's Southern White Cornbread.

2 eggs
2 cups of buttermilk
¼ ounces of oil
2½ cups of white corn meal
1 tsp of salt
1 tsp of butter

Instructions.

1. Preheat oven to 400 degrees.
2. Mix ingredients together.
3. Grease baking pan.
4. Bake for 30 minutes or until browned until your liking.

Note: Southern cornbread is always made with white cornbread and has a nuetral flavor. It's never sweet. Yellow cornmeal is considered sweet. Southerner's consider any cornbread that has sugar in it cake or some kind of muffin.

BBQ Tip: Whenever you are grilling out, no matter if it's Texas brisket or beer injected turkey and want to know if your food is done then use a thermometer. This is a foolproof way to know if your food has reached the target temperature for a period of time without cutting into the meat.

DAVID SLOCUM

Whole Animal Barbecue

Horse Trough Whole Hog.

There are several different methods to roasting a pig. All methods work, it's a question of style and taste. Barbecuing a whole hog is a Sun Brewing ritual. Barbecuing the entire beast is the ultimate ceremonious gathering for friends and family.

This is something I come up with derived from the idea of Trash Can Chicken. This is my favorite method in roasting a whole pig.

What I'm about to write will probably cause a lot of criticism but I believe it to be true because of experience and experimentation. All the evidence I have supports this conclusion;

<u>WHOLE PIGS TURN OUT BETTER WHEN FROZEN.</u>

When a pig is frozen it turns out juicer and more tender. I get my pig straight from the pig farmer and have him gut it the day before delivery or day of delivery. The fresher the pig the better.

Prepping Whole Hog.

1. Order fresh pig gutted and shaved ready to barbecue.
2. Clean entire pig with water to ensure all hair and dirt is off of the pig.
3. At a minimum rub salt all over the pig and any other rub of your preference.

4. Beer inject pig every few inches or so. The more injections the better.
5. Freeze the pig for a couple of days or until ready to barbecue.

Purify Horse Trough.

1. Clean horse trough with soap and water just like you would your pots and pans.
2. Sanitize horse trough by using sanitizer like StarSan or by burning it.

I did both. I also burned my initial coals for my pig barbecues inside the horse trough. I put a layer of pecan wood inside the horse trough and fired it up to create the low heat coals. I scooped out the glowing embers with a shovel into metal buckets and to the far sides of my barbecue pit.

Note: I took out the plastic spigot for draining the horse trough. You unscrew it. I also put in a metal flow off hose that I had on hand used in brewing. Any metal ball value or something comparable will work. I bought it from my local home brewing supplies store. This stainless steel blow off tube can be used for a thermometer. You can also plug it up with something to keep smoke inside for slow barbecue.

Building Pig Bed.

This is basically where you are going to lay the pig to roast for a good 20 to 24 hours.

1. Build perimeter using foot long cement blocks at 4 blocks wide and 8 blocks long at least one block high. Adjust to your pig size and your horse trough.
2. Lay thick layers of aluminum foil on the ground in the middle of the perimeter at least a couple feet longer and wider than your horse trough.
3. Get at least two cement blocks and position them in parallel to the length of the pig in the middle of the aluminum foil.
4. Put a layer of chicken wire over the cement blocks for the pig to lay on. You can purify this by adding the chicken wire to the horse trough when burning the wood to embers.
5. I put 4 pieces of pecan wood on each corner for support and I also put apple wood chunks in the cement block holes underneath the chicken wire.
6. Add large foil pan underneath chicken wire filled with beer and apple wood chunks.

Whole Hog Horse Trough Barbecue.

SUN BREWING COMPANY COOKBOOK SECOND EDITION

1. Make layers of glowing embers enough to cover the perimeter of the horse trough and to cover the entire top of the horse trough. This will take several hours.
2. Lay the frozen pig in the pig bed that has been centered on the aluminum foil.
3. Place the sanitized horse trough over the pig.
4. Shovel glowing low heat embers around the perimeter of the horse trough. This should be completely around the horse trough in a thick layer of embers.
5. Shovel glowing embers on top of horse trough to completely cover the top of the horse trough.
6. Keep making soft glowing embers all day and all night and keep putting them around and on top of the horse trough as the embers turn into ash. You want to ensure that there is always heat from soft glowing embers around and on top of the horse trough.

7. You can occasionally check the ambient temperature inside the horse trough with a thermometer.

Barbecue whole pig for approximately 20 to 24 hours around 200 degrees. Between 200 and 250 degrees is ideal.

I wouldn't go lower than 200 or higher than 250 but that's a personal preference because I go for an internal temperature from the pig of at least 185. Some people go lower temperatures but you risk not cooking completely. It's okay to go higher than 250 degrees ambient temperature however you are going to cook it quicker which means you could have dried it up a bit. If you hear a grease cracking sound then you need to pull the pig immediately because it's beginning to get over cooked.

If your pig cooks too quickly for whatever reasons then it's nothing a little mop sauce couldn't remedy but nothing is as good as an extremely juicy pig with crisp skin.

Keys to roasting a pig.

1. Keep internal pig temperature at a minimum of 180 degrees. Check the internal temp at different parts of the pig occasionally and be sure to check the deepest part of the pig.
2. Drink a craft beer.
3. Never put direct heat.
4. Always shovel the soft glowing embers to the sides layered against the walls.
5. Build small fire pits away from the pig to not affect ambient heat around the pig.

6. It can be tricky keeping a steady internal temperature. If it gets too hot then shovel out some coals or use a squirt gun to tame down the heat from the embers.

Also to keep the embers going... always have a fire pit going with coals ready to shovel.

Pulling Some Pork and Pig Head Tacos.

Pulling some pork and serving it up.

Pig Head Tacos.

Cook with passion but use the head too, Pig Head that is.

You can do a lot with the salty savory taste of Pig Head like use pearl barley as a topping along with endless other combinations. There are a lot of creative possibilities. In this case, the pig head is straight from the pig roast with very juicy soft unmatched savory flavor that reaches the salty, crunchy skin, and different tender umami parts of the of the head.

Goat Roast.

Roasting a goat is an ancient lineage and every culture has some version of it. Its flavor can be a little gamey but it's tender and delicious. It's perfect for special occasions, just add a little spice like a pinch of garam masala.

Keys to roasting a Goat.

1. Marinate in beer and salt and any other desired spices for one hour per pound with 1 cup of salt per gallon.
2. Sprinkle spices to taste. I tend to use salt and a pinch of garam masala. Let sit for an hour or two.
3. Keep ambient temperature at a minimum of 180 degrees and a maximum of 225. I typically go for 185 degrees with a goat. It normally takes approximately 6 hours to cook falling off the bone tender.
4. Drink a craft beer.
5. Never put direct heat.
6. Always shovel the soft glowing embers to the sides layered against the walls if you're using a horse trough method. If you have a larger enough grill then use indirect heat.
7. Build small fire pits away from the goat to not affect ambient heat around the goat, if using horse trough method. Use indirect heat for a grill.

8. If it gets too hot then shovel out some coals or use a squirt gun to tame down the heat from the embers.

Also to keep the embers going... always have a fire pit going with coals ready to shovel.

Carving some goat and Tacos de Cabeza.

Carving some goat and serving it up.

Goat Head Tacos - Tacos de Cabeza.

You can put a layer of basting olive oil if you like for extra seasoning. A good combination would be salt, pepper and cumin infused into olive oil then baste the head before cutting chunks off for Tacos de Cabeza.

For these tacos not much is needed, except tortillas and salsa. Flour or corn goes well with this taco.

Goat head has unique umami taste and will be one of the most unique tacos you'll ever enjoy. Tacos de Cabeza is a great idea. The real exquisite nature of the goat head is succulent with different textures from the seasoned crisp skin with different layers of mild savory flavors.

Everything Else.

Soups.

Stout Beer Goat Stew.

People really love this stew because of its unique taste and its festive nature. One I cooked it outside with kegs of stout beer. Everyone was willing to try it, and once they tried it... they loved it!

1 goat, cleaned and gutted
½ lb. of Hatch green chiles
1 large bag of potatoes
2 bags of carrots, sliced
1 bag whole carrots
1 keg of stout beer
3 oz. salt and pepper
3 oz. of minced garlic

Instructions.

1. Marinate goat in beer and salt overnight.
2. Put goat into 30-gallon stock pot or larger.
3. Fill stock pot with 15 gallons of stout beer and 5 gallons of water.
4. Lightly boil for an hour.
5. Dump the rest of the ingredients into the boil and cook for at least another 30 minutes.
6. Occasionally taste to see if you like it. You can water down or add more beer.

Note: I didn't use the goat head in this soup, but that would be a great idea—Goat Head Soup!
Suggested Beer Pairing:
Angels' Share Foreign Extra Stout
Ard Draoi Irish Red

Beer & Barley Oxtail Soup.

I grew up on oxtail soup... and I love it so much! My Grandpa Slocum was a U.S. Marine WWII combat vet and fought in many battles in the Philippines and some famous battles in Japan. Grandpa was also a butcher after his military service. He would bring home some nice cuts of meat or throwaways like oxtails—my father always got those.

I grew up on oxtail soup when it wasn't so fashionable. Back then oxtails were not sold, there were thrown away. I carry these little memories with me and for all my life. I remember just being five years old eating oxtail soup.

This recipe isn't quite what I grew up on, but it's in the same spirit. It is a very basic oxtail soup with a little beer and spice.

>4 lbs. of oxtails
>11 oz. of pearl barley
>1 oz. of salt and pepper
>4 pints beer (I tend to go for amber or brown ales, but you can never go wrong with porters or stouts)
>1 yellow onion sliced

1 tsp. oregano
2 bay leaves
1 cup flour

Instructions.

1. Sprinkle salt and pepper on oxtails.
2. Roll oxtails in flour. Make sure they are fully covered in flour.
3. Sautee oxtails with beer until golden and a brown.
4. Set aside oxtails and make thick gravy from same pan with stout, oxtail broth, and more flour. Make sure gravy is super thick.
5. Add all ingredients to stock pot on low heat.
6. Cook for at least 3 hours to get oxtails nice and tender and soup nice and thick.

Suggested Beer Pairing:
Same beer used in making the soup.

Brewer's Barley Bread Bowl.

This is my Brewer's bread cut into a bowl for a beer soup made with barley, onions, and beer-nuts. It's a very simple recipe but don't let that fool you! It's delish.

1 sweet onion cut in half and long sliced
11 oz. of pearl barley
Ramekin of beer-nuts

Note: Each brewer's bread will be different depending on the spent grains from the beer made. See Breads.

Instructions.

1. Choose a beer for your soup. In this case I used a porter. Ambers, browns, and porters all go well with this recipe.
2. In a saucepan on medium heat, cook the sweet onions in beer until soft for approximately 20 minutes.
3. Add a box (about 11 oz.) of pearl barley to the porter and onion saucepan at the 20-minute mark and continue to cook for another 5 minutes, then put on low heat to simmer.
4. Scoop into bread bowl.
5. Top bread bowl with beer-nuts. *Optional*: Add shredded cheddar cheese.

Suggested Beer Pairing:
Use the same beer you made the soup with.

Beer Nuts Cereal.

There are many ways to make beer-nuts. You could add mesquite flour or add brown sugar to the cooking process. I've had good results with all of the above and more.

32 oz. of fine milled spent grains
1 pint of beer
1 cup of Buñuelo seasoning (pure can sugar and ground cinnamon mixture)
1 tsp. of baking soda
1 tsp. of salt

Instructions.

1. Preheat oven to 300° F.
2. Combine all ingredients in a bowl and mix.
3. Spread evenly over baking sheet.
4. Bake for 45 minutes or until golden and brown.
5. Pull out baking sheet and let cool.

6. Break into chunks and pulse in blender. You want it chunky but not ground.
7. Serve in bowl of beer or milk.

Note: Any brewer would know how to mill some grains. Set it on the lowest setting to get the finest possible flour.

Suggested Beer Pairing:

Use the same beer you used to make the beer nuts with.

13

Salads.

Salads.

Chilendrina.

This dish is from Juarez, Mexico. However, I don't know if it originated there. It has unique flavors of pickled sourness and spice from a vinegar-based hot sauce.

Flour chicharrones
Shredded cabbage
Cueritos (thin strips of pork skin)
Tomato

Mexican sour cream
Avocado slices
Hot sauce
Instructions.

1. Take a sheet of flour chicharrones and spread cabbage all over it very generously.
2. Take a hand full of cueritos and spread them over the cabbage.
3. Sprinkle a handful of diced tomatoes over the cabbage and cueritos.
4. Top with slices of avocado.
5. Drizzle Mexican sour cream over it all.
6. Drizzle hot sauce over it all.
7. Serve with hot sauce and lime wedges.

Note: I always use Valentina hot sauce. You could, of course, add more ingredients, like sliced onions.

Suggested Beer Pairing:
Avocado Sour Ale
Meados de Alien Lager

Brewer's Salad.

I love this salad; there is a lot you can do it. You could also add pearl barley and/or a stout-reduction syrup dressing. Lots of good stuff with this versatile salad. You could also add dried brewer's bread as a topping.

Swiss chard

Kale

Beer nuts

Jalapeño-stuffed olives

Garlic-stuffed olives

Portobello mushrooms stuffed with spinach and white cheddar

Grilled oranges

Fried green heirloom tomatoes

Cherry peppers

Sun-dried red tomatoes

Sautéed asparagus and red onions

Instructions.

1. Layer Swiss chard and kale over salad bowl.
2. Mix the rest of the ingredients and sprinkle over Swiss chard and kale.
3. Place the large portobello-stuffed mushroom in the center of the salad bowl.
4. Sprinkle beer-nuts on top.

5. Top with a vinaigrette like my Blood Orange IPA Poppy Seed dressing (see Dressings).

Suggested Beer Pairing:
Tepache IPA
Le Cygne Noir Black Saison

14

Dressings.

Dressings.

Tepache & Olive Oil Dressing.

2 oz. of Tepache Vinegar (see Sauces) or apple cider vinegar
2 oz. of cilantro
6 oz. of olive oil

Instructions.

Put ingredients into a flip top bottle and shake. (See, some of my recipes are easy.)

Blood Orange IPA Poppy Seed Dressing.

1 oz. of olive oil
1 tsp. of poppy seeds
3 oz. of hazy IPA
1 oz. of freshly squeezed blood orange juice
1 tsp. of malt vinegar

Instructions.
Combine ingredients and shake.

15

Sides.

Sides.

Brisket Elote Beer Crinkle Fries.

Beer
Brisket (see below)

Beer Crinkle Fries (see below)
Mexican corn in a cup

Instructions.

1. Pull some brisket chunks and put them in a bowl topped with brisket juices. Set aside.
2. Put crinkle fries in a bowl and then put the brisket chunks all over the crinkle fries.
3. Top with Mexican Corn-in-a-Cup (see below) and cilantro.
4. Serve with side of lime wedge and hot sauce.

Brisket.

The best brisket is smoking from the instructions in my brisket section, but I realize it can be impractical for a lot of people. Here is a more practical, oven-roasted option if you are low on time.

Instructions.

1. Preheat oven to 300° F.
2. Sprinkle salt and pepper all over the brisket generously.
3. Place in baking pan with at least 1 inch of beer.
4. Roast for 2½ hours uncovered.
5. Uncover the brisket and roast for another 2½ hours or until succulent.

Beer Crinkle Fries.

> Beer
> 1 lb. of potatoes
> Canola oil
> Salt
> **Instructions.**

1. Preheat canola oil to 375° F in a deep fryer.
2. Wash potatoes. I don't peel them; I like a little skin on the edges.
3. Slice potatoes like thick waffle fry chips, approximately ½ inch to 1 inch thick. You'll need a waffle fry slicer.
4. Then use the same waffle slicer to cut the thick waffle-sliced chips the long way to make crinkle fry strips.
5. Soak crinkle fries in stout beer for at least 30 minutes.
6. Deep fry for approximately 10 minutes or until golden and brown.
7. Pull out fries and let dry on paper towels. Then season with salt and anything else you like. If you like spicy, then use a little chile.

Note: If you wanted to oven-bake beer crinkle fries, then preheat oven to 350° F. Bake for approximately 45 minutes to an hour or until as gold and brown as you like them.

Mexican Corn-in-a-Cup

> 32 oz. of corn (approximately 8 corn cobs)

1 cup of butter
1 cup Mexican cream
1 cup cotija cheese
1 tsp. of chile
Salt
Valentina hot sauce
Instructions.

1. Boil corn cobs for 5 minutes then simmer for another 5 minutes or until tender.
2. Strain corn and put into saucepan lightly coated with vegetable oil. Mix with salt, then cover pan.
3. Scoop a cup of corn into a 12 oz. glass.
4. Add 1 tsp. of butter and mix until melted.
5. Sprinkle with chile powder all over the top.
6. Drizzle Mexican cream.
7. Drizzle Valentina hot sauce.
8. Sprinkle generous amount of cotija cheese.
9. Serve with lime wedge.

Suggested Beer Pairing:
Use the same beer you used to make the dish with.
Gypsy Dude IPA

Sour Beer & Salt Potato Chips.

These potato chips are a hidden gem! Sour beer adds a beautiful complexity to the potato chips. The beer flavor is mild, but it's there. A lot of times beer is the ultimate food enhancer with a twist. It can be better than salt!

Sour beer
1 large potato
Canola oil
Salt
Instructions.

1. Preheat canola oil in a deep fryer to 350° F.
2. Wash potatoes and peel them if you like. I think a nice thin-sliced potato chip with skin around it is nice.
3. Slice potatoes with mandolin on thinnest setting. They should be thin sliced.
4. Soak potato slices in sour beer for at least 30 minutes. The longer the better. Hours are better than minutes.
5. Deep fry for approximately 5 minutes or until golden and a brown.
6. Pull out chips and let dry on paper towels. Season with salt.

Note: If you wanted to oven bake beer chips, then preheat

oven to 350° F. Bake for approximately 15 minutes or until as gold and brown as you like them.

Suggested Beer Pairing:

Use the same beer you used to make the dish with.

Narama Ancho Chile Sour Ale

Ana's Drunken Charro Beans.

A must try, so good!

2 lbs. of pinto beans
Approximately 80 oz. of Vienna lager
7 oz. of pickled jalapeños
1 lb. of bacon
16 oz. of bologna, cut into squares
16 oz. of ham, cut into squares
10 oz. of cracklings
1 can of pickled jalapeños
20 oz. of chorizo
16 oz. of sliced winnies (that's El Paso for hotdogs)

Instructions.

1. After rinsing pinto beans, put in crock pot with beer.
2. Cook bacon in frying pan. Make it nice and crispy, approximately 10 minutes on low heat. Save bacon grease.
3. Fry bologna in bacon grease.
4. Fry ham in bacon grease.
5. Fry winnies in bacon grease.
6. Cook chorizo in frying pan for approximately 5 minutes or so until browned.
   Note: Another thing I do a lot is to cook the meat in beer in the frying pan to caramelize. This is optional.
7. Put all ingredients into crock pot, mix, and cook until the beans are soft.

Note: You can do all this in a stock pot, too.
Suggested Beer Pairing:
Meados de Alien Lager
Atreyu Belgian Ale

16

Beer Breads

Beer Breads.

Sun Brewing's Stout Beer Tortillas.

2 cups of flour
1 tsp. of lard
1 tsp. of salt
½ cup of warm stout beer
Instructions.

1. Mix ingredients in a bowl to form dough.
2. Knead dough into a smooth ball.
3. Cover dough and let rest for an hour.
4. Grab a small handful of dough and roll into a ball. Use

a rolling pin if you like. I find using a beer bottle works just fine to rolling out the dough. You'll need to experiment a bit to see what handful you grab is the size you want. It doesn't take much dough to roll out a 5- or 6-inch flour tortilla. I'll make them about fajita-sized.
5. Heat up cast iron pan, comal, skillet, or whatever you're going to use to medium heat.
6. Place flour tortilla in cast iron pan and cook until the dough starts to bubble a bit, then flip to cook the other side. It takes roughly 60–90 seconds.

Suggested Beer Pairing:
Cheeky Devil Tropical Stout
Symposius Sour Porter

Pale Ale Pretzels.

These Pale Ale Pretzels are to die for! Absolutely delicious with a chewy, salty, beer flavor. One of my favorites for a party.

1 packet of active dry yeast
5 cups of all-purpose flour
1 egg
1 pint of warm pale ale
1 tsp. of sugar
1 oz. of salted butter
Egg wash and kosher salt.

Instructions.

1. Put warm beer in mixing bowl and add yeast.
2. Let beer and yeast mix sit for 15 minutes or until the bubblies form.
3. Mix in slowly the rest of the ingredients while on the lowest setting on your mixer.
4. Knead dough for approximately 5 minutes or until smooth.
5. Shape into dough ball and cover with plastic wrap.
6. Let dough sit for 1 hour or until doubled in size.
7. Preheat oven to 400° F.
8. Grease a cast-iron pan or a baking sheet.
9. Divide the dough into equal pieces or the different sizes you want.
10. Roll the dough into a rope shape.
11. Hold one end of the rope with one hand and the other end with your other hand to form a "U" shape.
12. Twist the two ends around each other.
13. Then fold the crossed ends down to the bottom to form the pretzel shape.
14. Place pretzels in cast-iron pan.

15. Baste egg wash on pretzels and sprinkle kosher salt over them.
16. Bake for 20 to 25 minutes or until golden and brown.

Note: A lot of people take a 2- or 3-quart pot of boiling water with a cup of baking soda and dip the pretzels for 15 to 30 seconds before baking. I don't do this step, but it gives the pretzels an extra shine and texture. I generally find the egg wash adequate for this.

Suggested Beer Pairing:
Left Turn at Albuquerque Pale Ale
Sun Black Ice Lager

Saison Fougasse.

4 cups of all-purpose flour
1 packet of active dry yeast
½ pint of saison
2 tsp. of melted butter

1 tsp. of sea salt
1 tsp. of sugar
1 tsp. of orange zest
1 tsp. of anise

Instructions.

1. Pour warm beer into mixing bowl with yeast and let sit for 15 minutes or until the bubblies form.
2. Put the mixer on the lowest setting and mix in the rest of the ingredients.
3. Once everything's mixed, turn up the speed a notch or two and mix for approximately 5 minutes or until smooth.
4. Shape dough into a ball and cover with plastic wrap.
5. Let dough sit for approximately 1 hour or until doubled in size.
6. Preheat oven to 350° F.
7. Punch the dough down to get the gas bubbles out, then split the dough into halves or thirds.
8. Shape into oval-like shape similar to a plant leaf.
9. Cut out sections of the dough to look leaf shaped. I like a maple leaf shape.
10. Let the dough rise for another 30 minutes or so until you like the shape rising.
11. Place fougasses on baking sheet and baste with olive oil.
12. Sprinkle with sea salt.
13. Bake for approximately 45 minutes or until golden and brown.

Suggested Beer Pairing:
Saison de Membrillo
Le Cygne Noir Black Saison

Brewer's Bread.

1½ cup of bread flour
1 cup of Hungarian wheat flour
1 cup of spent grain
1 packet of instant yeast
1 oz. of salted butter
1 egg
12 oz. of beer (the same beer from the spent grain)

Instructions.

1. Add warm beer and yeast and let sit for 15 minutes or until the bubblies form.
2. Add the rest of the ingredients slowly with the mixer on its lowest setting.

3. Then knead on a higher setting for 5 minutes or so until smooth.
4. Shape dough into a ball, cover with plastic wrap, and let sit for 1 hour or until dough has doubled in size.
5. Preheat oven to 350° F.
6. Slash bread to make a smiley face.
7. Bake for 45 minutes.

Suggested Beer Pairing:
Use the same beer that you used for making the bread.

17

Sauces.

Sauces.

Sun Brewing's Beer Mustard.

- 7 tsp. mustard powder
- 2 tsp. yellow mustard seeds
- 2 tsp. brown mustard seeds

1 tsp. garlic salt
1 tsp. ground onion
1 tsp. turmeric
1 tsp. ground piloncillo
> 1 tsp. Tepache Vinegar (see Sauces) or apple cider vinegar

2 oz. of pale ale

Instructions.

1. Take 1 tsp. yellow and 1 tsp. brown mustard seeds and grind them into a powder. Set the rest of the seeds aside.
2. Mix remaining ingredients in a blender or by hand.
3. Fill a saucepan with a couple of inches of water.
4. Place mustard in a bowl large enough to fit over the saucepan.
5. Heat saucepan on low heat and mix the mustard. Add in the rest of the mustard seeds. Mix until it thickens, approximately 5 minute.
6. Pour into a sanitized jar.

Sun Brewing's Beer Mole

1 cup Animal crackers
5 Tsp. Sesame seeds
5 Tsp. Pumpkin seeds
5 Tsp. Peanuts
2 cloves Garlic
5 Guajillo chiles
5 Pasilla chiles

5 Ancho chiles
2 oz. Chile pequin
1 tablet (3 oz.) Abuelita Mexcian chocolate
2 Caldo do res packets (you can buy these seasoning packets in Mexican grocery stores)
Beer (I'll typically use a pint of Vienna lager or brown ale)
Instructions.

1. Fire up grill with briquettes.
2. Once coals are glowing embers over medium heat, add pecan wood.
3. In a cast-iron pan, spread out animal crackers, peanuts, sesame seeds, pumpkin seeds, and one garlic clove evenly.
4. Roast animal cracker mix on low until toasted, approximately 15 minutes.
5. In a separate cast-iron pan, roast the chiles. Spread out chiles evenly.
6. Take animal cracker mix from grill and put in blender with chicken broth and puree.
7. Put animal cracker mix back into the cast-iron pan and add 1 tablet Abuelita Mexican chocolate.
8. Mix 2 caldo de res seasoning packets into the animal cracker mix.
9. Take stems off of roasted chiles and take seeds out.
10. Blend all the chiles with beer.
11. Strain chiles.
12. Take the liquid from the strained chiles and mix into pot with the animal cracker mix.

13. Stir it up good and let it slow cook on the grill for approximately 15 minutes or until desired consistency.

Sun Brewing's Green Mole.

1 pint of Vienna lager
3 bay leaves
6 tomatillos
3 cabbage leaves
½ cup of pumpkin seeds
½ cup of sesame seeds
1 serrano pepper
2 poblano peppers
1 tsp. of cumin
1 crushed garlic clove
1 small white onion
1 cilantro bunch
Salt and pepper

Instructions.

1. Toast pumpkin and sesame seeds for a few minutes until slightly browned.
2. Roast tomatillos in open aluminum foil over grill until charred and soft.
3. Heat frying pan on low heat with lard.
4. Cut stems off of chiles.
5. Blend ingredients, including beer.
6. Pour into frying pan and cook for 30 minutes or until thickness desired.

Note: For brewing beer using green mole as an adjunct don't use any grease and only use beer and take out seeds of chiles and puree sauce. With regular green mole you can pulse it and keep it with seeds, thick and chunky as you like.

Sun Brewing's Tamarindo Salsa.

A beautiful blend of beer salsa. The tropical fruit balances out the tamarind's tartness, and the unique sweet citrus and tart flavors balance the smoky heat of the chiles. The beer enhances everything.

Tamarindo sauce
½ yellow onion, diced
3 jalapeños, diced
Diced fruit
Garlic
Guajillo chile
Pasilla chile
Ancho chile
Chile pequin
Chicken broth

Instructions.

1. Fire up grill with briquettes.
2. Once coals are glowing embers over medium heat, add mesquite wood chunks.
3. In a cast-iron pan, place onions and garlic clove and drizzle olive oil over it. Roast for approximately 30 minutes.

4. In a separate cast-iron pan, roast the chiles. Spread out chiles evenly until charred, approximately 30 minutes.
5. Take stems off of roasted chiles and take seeds out.
6. Blend all the ingredients with chicken broth.
7. Strain chiles.
8. Dice grilled papaya, yellow onion, and jalapeños and put into tamarindo sauce.
9. Put salsa back on the grill and mix in tamarindo sauce. Let it slow cook on the grill for approximately 15 minutes or until desired thickness.

Once the salsa is done cooking, add some diced fruit. I normally use diced mango, diced pineapple, or papaya.

Grilled Papaya.

1. Cut papaya in half and take out the seeds.
2. Grill over medium heat, flesh-side down until charred, about 1 minute.
3. Flip papaya over, sprinkle with brown sugar, and let slightly caramelize.

Porter Tamarindo Sauce.

1 cup of tamarinds
1 pint of porter
Instructions.

1. Peel and seed tamarind pods.

2. Wash tamarinds.
3. Lightly boil tamarinds in beer for 15 minutes.
4. Strain tamarinds. You'll need to push some of it through. Discard the remainder.
5. Blend the thick tamarind paste in a blender with a little beer. Use your judgement; it's usually around 4 oz. You'll want it like a BBQ-sauce thickness.

Note: You can add sugar and spice if you like to give it other flavors, like sweet and tangy.

Sun Brewing's Chamoy Sauce.

1 lemon
1 lime
1 orange
1 lb. dried apricots
> 3 pinches of El Guapo chile mix (you can buy El Guapo seasonings at your local Mexican grocery store)

3 pinches of hot chile mix
Half piloncillo cone
½ cup of Jamaica (hibiscus)
1 quart of Vienna lager
1 shot of mezcal
Instructions.

1. Dump apricots, Jamaica, and piloncillo into a pot with the beer.

2. Boil beer mix for 15 minutes.
3. Dump sauce into blender, then add salt and ground chiles.
4. Freshly squeeze orange, lemon, and lime into blender.
5. Add 1 shot of mezcal.
6. Blend until you have a saucy consistency.

Sun Brewing's Green Chamoy Sauce.

1 lemon
1 lime
1 orange
1 lb. dried apricots
2 oz. of Hatch green chile puree
3 oz. of pure cane sugar
2 oz. of pickle juice
1 quart of American lager

Instructions.

1. Dump apricots and sugar into a pot with the beer.
2. Boil beer mix for 15 minutes.
3. Dump sauce into blender, then add pickle juice and green chiles.
4. Freshly squeeze orange, lemon, and lime into blender.
5. Blend until you have a saucy consistency.

Sun Brewing's Beer BBQ Sauce.

1 tsp. of smoked paprika

1 tsp. of celery salt

1 tsp. of ginger

3 oz. of Sun Brewing Mole sauce

1 oz. tamarind paste

½ cup of Sun Brewing Beer Mustard (see above)

Note: Substitute one tablet from a 19 oz. package of Abuelita Mexican chocolate for the Mole sauce if you want to tone down the spice.

Instructions.

Mix all ingredients in a saucepan on low heat and simmer for 5 minutes.

Sun Brewing's Hog Sauce.

Ingredients.
2 Quarts of Amber Ale
2 quarts of Tepache vinegar
1 ounce of kosher salt
2 ounces of Cayenne pepper
2 ounces of achiote chile (or El Guapo chile mix)
2 ounces of Chamoy sauce

Instructions.
Mix well.

Note: You can do a lot with this sauce to make into a specific bbq sauce whether it's adding mustard and taking out chamoy or adding ketchup and honey.

Stout Beer Ganache.

1. Add 1 pint of stout beer to a saucepan and simmer on low heat.
2. Add in the Abuelita Mexican chocolate one tablet at

a time until all melted or until consistency desired. It generally takes about half the 19 oz. package.

Note: Another great idea is a stout beer reduction...or stout beer glaze! For stout beer reduction, add your beer to a saucepan on low heat and simmer until reduced by half or desired thickness. Add a sweetener like maple syrup or honey for glaze.

Tepache Vinegar.

You will need to take the tepache recipe and procedure and let it ferment longer to turn into vinegar.

See recipe and procedure for how to make Tepache.

1. Ferment tepache for at least 3 weeks, then taste it to see if you like it.
2. If you don't like the taste then let it ferment longer, probably another week.
3. If you like it, then boil it and bottle it.

Note: As with all fermentations, be sure all equipment is sanitized.

Beverages.

Tepache.

Pineapple skins from 1 pineapple
Piloncillo—2 cones of 8 oz. each (If you do not have piloncillo then use brown sugar.)
2 cinnamon sticks
5 cloves

Instructions.

1. Cut the skins off of the pineapple and rinse them.
2. Place the ingredients in a clay pot with 2 quarts of mineral water. *Note*: I love Topo Chico mineral water which is a softer tasting and in my view the best tasting mineral water. Use the water that tastes good to you, spring water is a good choice.
3. Cover clay pot with cheesecloth and let it ferment at room temperature for 3 days.
4. Strain ingredients out of clay pot, put the tepache beverage in a pitcher, cap it, and place in the refrigerator. This is a live beverage, meaning it will keep fermenting if you take it out of the fridge. It should be drunk within a few days.

Note: You can let ferment longer than three days, but five days is the longest I'll let it ferment because each day after five days it starts to taste too much like vinegar.

Russian Kvas.

10 loafs of rye bread
1 cup of honey
1 cup of raisons
5 sprigs of mint
Instructions.

1. Let 5 loaves of rye bread dry out overnight.
2. Put the dried-out loaves of bread and other ingredients in the 5-gallon brewing bucket.
3. Fill with warm tap water (approximately 80 to 90° F). *Note:* Boil 4 gallons of water and use a Camden tablet, then let cool.
4. Cover with cheese cloth.
5. Let sit overnight or until thick foam is formed on top.
6. Stick in the fridge until ready to put into fermentation. Boil for 10 minutes before dumping in fermentation.

Atole.

Here is a quick recipe for atole to serve to friends.
2 quarts of water (add milk if desired)
1 piloncillo cone
2 cinnamon sticks
1 cup masa harina

Note: Add 1 or 2 tablets of Abuelita Mexican chocolate for **champurrado**—one tablet for mild chocolate or two for medium.

Instructions.

1. Mix masa harina (Mexican cornmeal), water, piloncillo, and cinnamon in a saucepan.
2. Simmer until desired thickness.
3. Add vanilla when finished heating.

Note: This atole recipe above was adapted for brewing beer; I make it thick.

For serving as a beverage you would add milk or water and serve a little thinner, soupier.

Calientito.

This is a Mexican Christmas fruit punch served traditionally for the Christmas holiday season.

2 lbs. of guyabas cut into quarters
2 lbs. of tecojotes

4 apples, chopped into cubes
4 peaches, chopped into cubes
2 lbs. of cana de azucar (the actual cane)
3 cinnamon sticks
Handful of Jamaica (hibiscus)
4 tamarinds
1 piloncillo cone
1 lb. of cirvela pasa (dried prunes)
4 pears, chopped up

Instructions.

1. Add cinnamon sticks and piloncillo to the calientito pot, which should be at least 2 gallons.
2. Boil cinnamon sticks and piloncillo with 1 gallon of water.
3. Boil Jamaica in a separate, at least 2-quart pot for 10 minutes.
4. Drain Jamaica water into a calientito pot of at least 2 gallons.
5. Add tecojotes and boil for 10 minutes.
6. Turn heat to medium low.
7. Add peaches, pears, apples, and pealed tamarinds.
8. Add water if you need to and boil for 15 minutes.
9. Add guayabas, cana de azucar, and cirvelas pasas. Ssimmer for 30 minutes.

Pappy Slocum's Beer Nog.

I named my beer nog that I drink for Christmas after

Joshua Slocum, who was the first to sail around the world alone and wrote a best-selling book about his adventures.

½ pint of Russian imperial stout
1 piloncillo cone
1½ cup of whole milk
½ cup of sweetened condensed milk
1 cup of heavy whipping cream
Vanilla extract
Cinnamon sticks
Ground cinnamon
Ground cloves
Ground nutmeg

Instructions.

1. Whisk milk, cream, two shakes of cinnamon, one pinch of cloves, two pinches of nutmeg together in a saucepan.
2. Add piloncillo and cook over medium heat until piloncillo is melted and combined, then simmer. Stir nog until thickness desired.

3. Add Russian imperial stout to serving glass, then top with nog.
4. Garnish with cinnamon stick and pinch of cinnamon or nutmeg.

18

Desserts.

Desserts.

Stout Chocoflan Cake

Absolutely decadent!
Flan blend (custard):
6 eggs
1 can la lechera (sweetened milk)
12 oz. of evaporated milk
1 box (8 oz.) of cream cheese at room temp

1 tsp. of almond extract
Cake mix:
1¾ cups flour
2 cups sugar
¾ cup unsweetened cocoa
1½ tsp. of baking soda
1½ tsp. of baking powder
1 tsp. of salt
2 eggs
1¼ cup of buttermilk
½ cup of butter
1 tsp. of vanilla extract
1 cup of hot stout beer
1 package of chocolate pudding
Cajeta (Mexican carmel)

Instructions.

1. Preheat oven to 370° F.
2. Blend all ingredients for flan and set aside.
3. For cake mix, use hand mixer to blend eggs, milk, melted butter, vanilla extract, and stout beer and set aside.
4. For the cake dry mix, use whisk to mix flour, sugar, cocoa, baking soda, baking powder, salt, and pudding mix.
5. Add wet ingredients to dry ingredients and mix with a hand mixer.
6. Add half an inch of cajeta at the bottom of a baking pan.
7. Add chocolate cake mix on top of the cajeta.
8. Then pour the flan on top. It will sink to bottom.

9. Do a Baño Maria bake, which means to have a deep baking pan filled with hot water and put the cake covered with aluminum foil into the hot water pan.
10. Bake for approximately 2 hours.

Suggested Beer Pairing:
Sun Arkhangelisk Russian Imperial Stout
You Don't Know Jack! Fruit IPA

Saison Ice Cream.

1 cup of saison ale
2 cups of whipping cream
½ cup of milk
1 egg
½ cup of pure cane sugar
Instructions.

1. Reduce beer by half in saucepan.
2. Mix in the rest of the ingredients and keep on low heat.
3. Use ice cream machine to churn or make ice cream by hand.
4. To make ice cream by hand, transfer to container and freeze.
5. Once custard starts to freeze, use a fork or sharp object and poke holes to break it up and mash it.
6. Repeat step 5 until you have smooth, creamy ice cream.

Note: This works great on a banana split!

DAVID SLOCUM

Beer Soufflé Ice Cream Sandwich.

This sandwich is to die for! Beautiful layers of beer in the soufflé with a light crust of beer-nuts. The saison ice cream is what makes this dessert over the top because of the combination of beer soufflé and ice cream. Decadent.

The spice garam masala is in there too... it's one of my all-time favorite spice combinations! I don't use it much because it's very powerful and it needs a special place. garam masala reminds me of how I've always wanted to learn Indian cuisine. Indian cuisine is one of the most underrated cuisines of the world. I hope to learn more of this cuisine, but I don't want my brain to explode! I'm still trying to blend beautiful combinations of beer flavors .

With my ingredients I normally always go for equal parts. For example, if I have 3 eggs then it'll be 3 egg whites to 3 egg yolks to 3 Tsps of flour to 3 Tsps of butter to 13 oz.s of beer.

1 Saison beer
4 tsp. of butter
4 eggs
4 tsp. of flour
2 pinches of garam masala

Instructions.

1. Preheat oven to 400° F.
2. Melt butter on low heat in a saucepan, then whisk flour into the butter.
3. Stir constantly until it thickens, approximately 3 minutes.
4. Put on low heat and stir in one beer and egg yolks and cook for 10 minutes.
5. Put egg whites in mixer and mix on high speed until nice and thick.
6. Take a scoop of egg whites and gently fold it into base mixture.
7. Then pour the entire mixture back into egg white bowl and gently fold a few times or so.
8. Pour soufflé mixture into baking containers.

9. Sprinkle parmesan cheese on top to form a layer of cheese.
10. Sprinkle beer-nuts on top of cheese.
11. Bake for 30 minutes.
12. Cut soufflé in half, then put a scoop or two of ice cream in the middle to make a sandwich. Do this quickly so that the soufflé melts the ice cream and is hot.

Optional: Add a beer molasses or some kind of sauce topping.

Suggested Beer Pairing:
Saison de Membrillo
Symposius Sour Porter

19

Final Thoughts.

In this cookbook, I have showcased the culinary tastes and culture of Sun Brewing and my Borderland Avant-Garde cuisine. Writing this and sharing these recipes and techniques has been a humbling experience for me, and I'm very grateful to you for taking an interest in the Sun Brewing story and in exploring the exciting flavors of my community and heritage.

Sun Brewing culture is eclectic, diverse, DIY, and come as you are. The picture below illustrates this; it was taken at Sun Brewing's annual Keg Party, a beer festival held on the Rio Grande.

Sun Brewing is a zoo; truly a place where poets, bards, artists, students, executives, doctors, lawyers, bikers, blue collar workers, and laborers can rub elbows around a shared love for beer, food, and the borderland—and that's what I love most about it.

Look at this book as not just a recipe book but as a book of food and beer stories meant to inspire you by example. Brewing and cooking is personal, so I hope I've helped you put your own taste buds to work so you can find your own culinary signature.

Taking Brewing from Hobby to Community.

How can you take your love of craft beer to the next level? There's nothing like educating yourself, learning a craft, and getting involved in a community.

Get to Know the Craft

I taught myself how to brew from reading books and from the University of Life. I've made award-winning beers, so I guess I know a little something of what I'm doing. The single biggest piece of advice I can give aspiring brewers is to read books. I read as many books as possible and I took notes so that I could become a better version of myself. The two books that are a must read for learning how to brew are *The*

Complete Joy of Home Brewing by Charlie Paapzian and *How To Brew by John Palmer.*

I personally think Charlie deserved a Pulitzer for *The Complete Joy of Home Brewing*. His contribution cannot be underestimated or even fully understood yet. Charlie's no worries philosophy, "Relax, don't worry, have a home brew," is perfect for many occasions beyond brewing your own beer. This approach paved the way for the American craft brewing revolution.

You can also join the American Homebrewers Association and your local homebrewing club.

History of Beer in El Paso

My Great Predecessors

According to texasbreweries.com there were these historic breweries registered.

The El Paso Brewing Association 1904-1918.
Harry Mitchell Brewing Co. 1935-1955
Falstaff Brewing Corp 1955-1967

According to the El Paso Historical Society, shortly after the repeal of Prohibition, Harry Mitchell born in England organized to start a new brewery with three other businessman. They named the brewery Harry Mitchell and it was built over the ruins of the Old El Paso Brewery.

I only wished I could have tasted Harry's Special Lager to see what it tasted like back then with their brewing equipment. My intuition tells me it would have been as good as or better than some giant beer companies of today. My gut feeling is that they would have made a full bodied and high quality beer. Eventually Falstaff bought them out but they had a good and historic run in the borderlands.

Now on to my great predecessor; **Jaxon's**. Jaxon's was truly revolutionary for El Paso because they added craft beer to their restaurant. A truly revolutionary thing to do back then and it's no small task or risk involved to make that happen. According to a local news article from KVIA Jaxon's restaurant was established in 1973. I also looked up Jaxon's brewing permit through the TABC and they had a registered brewing permit for their N. Mesa location from 1983 to 2011. That's a long time to be serving craft beer to El Paso. Jaxon's also won a gold medal in 1997 at the GABF. I looked up the Great American Beer Festival's historical records. What a great achievement for back in the day! Back then brewing knowledge was more esoteric and the iconic craft breweries of today were just getting started blazing their own trails to become the godfather's of craft beer. Jaxon's is what I would consider "The Godfather of Craft Beer in El Paso".

I was drinking craft beer at Jaxon's before I even knew what craft beer was. I would go to Jaxon's to eat their good food and have a beer way before I even knew the term "craft beer". Jaxon's was a full-fledged restaurant then added a brewing operation. That brewing operation had to have cultivated many local brewers! Albeit some brewers that brewed at Jaxon's went on to own or co-own breweries here in El Paso. Jaxon's truly helped cultivate a brewing environment here in

El Paso and helped pave the way for myself and others like me who had aspirations to brew.

Craft Beer Today

Jaxon's was the only thing in town for a long time. When Jaxon's closed there was really nothing, no craft beer being brewed in El Paso until Sun Brewing came along in 2014. When Sun Brewing opened we were the only craft brewery in all of El Paso at that time. Then came a beer boom around 2016.

July 5th 2014, Sun Brewing had its grand opening. When I opened, the only other brewery in close proximity was High Desert in Las Cruces, NM. High Desert is another revolutionary brewery that has been around a long time since 1997, according to lascruces.com. They were the only brewery around coupled with Jaxon's for a long time.

The first festival attended by Sun Brewing was the inaugural Brew at the Zoo on February 28th, 2015. I had my own craft beer festival on June 6th 2015 but it was more like a party. I named it "The Keg Party on the Rio". I invited other breweries to partake in my festivities too. I had a lot of fun gulping beer on the river. It was good times, beer, bbq and river raft races. I took some kegs and barbecued a pig on the river while people were swimming or in a raft kicken it. My vision was to have it organic so that it could grow on its own, for example, a flea market selling local products. I'll keep at it and see where it leads but it helps to have water in the river. I never understood why the water from the river was restricted in El Paso. There was no water in the river except for a few months of the year. I think there could be a billion dollar business boom if we just had the river full of water because that would lead to restaurants on the river, boats on the river and my kegs on the river!

The Sun City Craft Beer Festival is the oldest craft beer festival in El Paso, which kicked off its first festival on Saturday September 28th, 2013. One of the organizers of The Sun City Craft Beer Festival was by Nahum Avila. In my view, this was extremely important in the History of Craft Beer in El Paso because it brought people together in celebration of craft beer in a way nobody else could up to that point in time. The Sun City Craft Beer festival also brought awareness to the entire city about craft beer, including future business owners.

Then a couple of breweries were racing to open next after me: Ode and Deadbeach. They both had their grand openings essentially within a month of each other at the end of 2015. Ode at the end of September and Deadbeach in early November 2015. These two breweries were planting their flag to be that flagship brewery of El Paso. Ode was one of the best Brewpub's in Texas. Albert Salinas the co-owner and head brewer at Ode made excellent beer. You take that coupled with a good chef named Norbert Portillo and you have one of the very best Brewpubs in Texas. Deadbeach had a couple of brewers Gabe Montoya and Justin Ordonez who met the Hunt's. It was a perfect marriage. The heart and soul brewers of Deadbeach met the business men – The Hunt's. They partnered with Jason Hunt. This was a perfect pairing because sometimes breweries lack the business experience and lack the funding to be successful. Deadbeach has the best of both worlds.

In 2016 was the first year the Sun City Craft Beer Festival showcased local breweries, Sun Brewing, Ode and Deadbeach. I remember thinking to myself, what a great day! El Paso has its own craft beer festival with its own local breweries. I distinctively remember thinking to myself of having a sense of pride being a part of it all.

El Paso Brewing Co opened about a year after Ode and Deadbeach. Carlos Guzman had some big shoes to fill having a name like El Paso Brewing Co. He named his brewery after the historic El Paso Brewing & Ice Co. The tables started to turn for the craft beer community in El Paso. The city was starting to get more and bigger craft breweries like other craft beer cities.

This same time period around 2016 you seen a beer boom not only in El Paso, but in Las Cruces and Juarez. According to the El Paso Times article from October 2019 - Juarez Craft Beer Scene Bubbling Over, "Hijos de la Guayaba, Border Brewing Co. and The Beer Box all opened in the past two years, since licensing rule changed." Juarez has a lot of breweries popping up nowadays and according to Erick Valverde one of the organizers of Juarez's craft beer festival Desertica, there are 30 registered breweries in Juarez. Erick Valverde – brewer and brewery owner is also one of the key organizers of Festival Desertica. That's truly amazing and a great thing having all those breweries contributing and serving Juarez. We all enrich each other in a lot of ways and craft beer is another great way for this. This was another great progression in the borderlands! Erick and his own brewery Valkyria did a clean sweep of gold medals for their wins. Blazing Tree Brewery won a bronze for their Pecan Porter and El Paso Brewery won a bronze for their Thunderbird Dark Lager and a gold for their Scottish Ale and Calvary Scout Stout. What a great way to kick off a new festival in the borderlands.

It's the same story in Mexico as it is in the United States regarding beer giants taking essentially the whole beer pie. I'm not against publicly traded companies but I am against manipulating the market to gain market share. We don't need monopolies, oligopolies or unfair practices. Unethical practices happen at all levels and not just from beer giants. The rules are changing and we have greater numbers of smaller guys brewing beer offering more diversity and that's what I love about it. I'm happy the rules continue to change for us small guys so we can continue to do what we love – make a living brewing beer. It's great to see the laws changing so that more breweries can open, not just in El Paso but in other cities in other countries as well.

The Sun City Mashers was established in May of 2016. Recognized club with the American Homebrewers Association since 2018. Key leaders still today and former presidents were Mike Stauffer and Richard Mojica. These two guys I know personally and I've always admired their devotion to craft beer. This club is extremely important and I think the importance can be overlooked sometimes. The Mashers have a good 30 members or so and have cultivated brewing culture and expertise. These Mashers are the future brewers in El Paso and future Brewery owners. Current club president Carlos Pomar almost won it all in the National Homebrew Competition advancing to the final round, but let's be honest here... with all the gazillions of people entering, there is really no difference between the top groups of brewers. I would hate to be the judge trying to figure out who wins a medal when there are several beers worthy of winning. I look forward to brewing with these Mashers especially Willie Montoya aka "Goat". These Mashers do it for the love of beer and brewing. I have a lot of respect for this club and look forward to brewing and sharing knowledge.

Blazing Tree Brewing opened sometime after El Paso Brewing in 2017. Blazing Tree Brewery has had a good influence in El Paso, not only with their own brewery but they've also influenced 3 other breweries to open that all were apart of Blazing Tree in some fashion at one point.

Aurelias Brewery opened in middle 2019 and was similar to the Jaxon's model of a full-fledged restaurant that makes their own beer. This would be slightly different than say Ode Brewing because Ode only had their own beer with their food.

Old Sheepdog Brewery opened in late 2019 in December. Old Sheepdog and a new wave of breweries opened right before the pandemic or during the pandemic.

Craft Rhythm & Brews, Mountain Star and Mission Trail Brewery all opened here recently during the pandemic. I wish them all the very best and I've met Fred from Craft Rhythm

& Brews. They are good people and its family owned. I think these breweries will have several great brewers come out of their establishments to continue their work.

The History of Beer in El Paso is fascinating and evolving. We can see the progression from macro-brewery standard commodities to microbreweries to 100% Spontaneous Farmhouse Ales brewed out of a bucket that are world class. It's exciting to see what the future holds for craft beer in El Paso. My feelings are we don't need to be like other cities, we just need to be who we are, do our passion, be proud of what we got and to cultivate our own true local craft beer culture.

Get to Know the People Who Make the Laws

We need our local and state leaders to be advocates for us brewers. It's an exciting adventure to build, own, and operate a brewery and restaurant, and our lawmakers have a lot of power to make it easier for us small business owners to get up and running. If you want to be part of the brewing community, you'll want to know who represents you and what laws are on the books—and how the law should change.

Good laws will promote brewing at all levels. Bad laws create red tape or other challenges for the small business owner. Here in Texas, for example, we have a legal distinction between a "beer" and an "ale" based on alcohol percentage. This is an absurd bureaucratic invention that defies science; all ales are beers, after all. Some folks use "beer" to mean "lager," but even that has to do with production method rather than ABV. It creates confusion without actually helping consumers or businesses.

We need laws that make sense and support us. Fractional distillation beer, also known as ice beer, is another example. Making an eisbock is illegal—or, technically, freeze concentrating beer is illegal. Presumably this has something to do with the high ABVs, but it isn't illegal to barrel age a beer and package it at 20% ABV. Doesn't make sense to have a law like that.

We need to be smarter about what we put into law.

I want to see legions of brewers making world-class beers out of a bucket! Everyone has to start somewhere, and laws should provide pathways that balance innovation with public safety. Texas is friendly to entrepreneurs, but we can do more with respect to the brewing industry. I would like to see people able to set up in their garage and sell beer out of their home—or at least produce it there. We need an environment conducive to the entrepreneurial spirit for everyone. Establishments are becoming standardized. I love a good gastropub, myself, but I .m want diversity like street food. Imagine one day if there were such a thing as street beer!

Giving Back.

Everything I got good in my life is a direct result of what I've did good to others.

I give back what I can, but I strive to give back more. Hopefully, one day I can be a great philanthropist.

It's been my policy since day one to offer free meals to anyone homeless or down on their luck and in need of a helping hand. It's not a handout, it's a hand up.

I'm very proud of Sun Brewing for this. I know what it's like to be down and out and feeling hopeless. I will help anyone who needs a hot plate.

I remember Arnold's 6 rules for success and giving back was one of them.

Arnold Schwarzenegger's 6 Rules for Success

I love Arnold so much! The Terminator... to the Governator! The Austrian immigrant, professional body builder, American actor, businessman, author, politician, and philanthropist has a lot to teach us (regardless of your politics). His Six Rules for Success keep me motivated as an entrepreneur and innovator.

1. Trust yourself.

Many young people are getting so much advice from their parents and from their teachers and from everyone. But what is most important is that you dig deep down and ask yourself, "Who do I want to be?" Not *what*, but *who*. Figure out for yourself what makes you happy, no matter how crazy it may sound to other people.

2. Break the Rules.

Break the rules—not the law, but the rules. It is impossible to be a maverick or a true original if you're too well behaved and don't at least try the things that others say can't be done. You have to think outside the box. After all, what is the point of being on this earth if all you want to do is be liked by everyone and avoid trouble?

3. Don't Be Afraid to Fail.

In anything I've ever attempted, I was always willing to fail. You can't always win, but don't be afraid of making decisions. You can't be paralyzed by fear of failure or you will never push yourself. You keep pushing because you believe in yourself and in your vision and you know that it is the right thing to do. Success will come!

4. Don't Listen to the Naysayers.

How many times have you heard that you can't do this and you can't do that and it's never been done before? I love it when someone says that no one has ever done this before, because then when I do it that means that I'm the first one. Pay no attention to the people that say it can't be done. I never listen to, "You can't." I always listen to myself when that little voice says, "Yes, you can."

5. Work Your Butt Off.

You never want to fail because you didn't work hard enough. Mohammed Ali, one of my great heroes, had a great line in the '70s when he was asked, "How many sit-ups do you do?" He said, "I don't count my sit-ups. I only start counting when it starts hurting. When I feel pain, that's when I start counting, because that's when it really counts." That's what makes you a champion. No pain, no gain.

But when you're out there partying, horsing around, someone out there at the same time is working hard. Someone is getting smarter, and someone is winning. Just remember that. Now, if you want to coast through life, don't pay attention to any of those rules. But if you want to win, there is absolutely no way around hard, hard work. Just remember, you can't climb the ladder of success with your hands in your pockets.

6. Give Back.

Whatever path that you take in your lives, you must always find time to give something back to your community, your state, or your country.

Remember these six rules. Trust yourself, break some rules, and don't be afraid to fail, ignore the naysayers, work like hell, and give something back.

Giving Thanks.

I dedicate this book to my family: my wife Ana and my kids, Natalie, Anita, and Jake, who fill my life with pure joy.

SUN BREWING COMPANY COOKBOOK SECOND EDITION

I wouldn't be where I am today without her—I love you equally! The first time she told me she loved me, I told her, "Equally." I told her I knew I loved her after three days and wanted to get married after three weeks. She said, "You're only saying that because I make great tortillas!" It actually took years to get married because she didn't believe me.

Thank you to all the people who have helped me along the way—and the list is long: my parents, my family, my friends… you are all family to me.

There were times throughout my entire life I needed help, from when I was a kid to a student in college to the military to today. Thanks to Saint and Tomcat, who kept me sane during my last combat tour in Iraq. Ooorah, Marines! Semper Fi!

DAVID SLOCUM

I want to thank my parents for helping me out way back when I had no vehicle and was broke in college. My parents worked extremely hard to provide a better life for me and my brothers. My parents worked the graveyard shift. My mother worked late nights in a meat factory, and my father worked third shift at a gas station when I was in pre-school. I've always been so very proud of where we came from and how much they have accomplished. My dad worked a full-time job and put himself through college while supporting a family. He is now a retired military officer. I always had a hot plate and roof over my head.

I want to write a big thank you to the brewing community, for I wouldn't have come this far without you.

Special thanks to Charlie Papazian, who is the founder of so many things, from the Brewer's Association to the American Homebrewers Association, and the author of *The Complete Joy of Home Brewing*. As it was for so many others, his was the book that taught me home brewing and initiated me into this wonderful world of craft and flavor.

Thank you.

I know Sun Brewing means something to you, know that you have always meant far more to me.

And to anyone who feels that their dreams are unattainable; they're not.

It's not the awards and accolades that truly matters... it's the relationships from the journey.

Thank you.

20

Letter to Fallen Marines.

Letter to Fallen Marines.

As a former-marine, I'm aware that I'm here, today, but there are a lot of good guys who are not. We don't always get a chance to express our love and appreciation for our fallen brothers, so I wanted to take the time now. Who knows if I'll ever have a better place to say this than right here?

It's been such a long road and a bit cold at times, but I've always believed there is light at the end of the tunnel. I'm grateful for every single day of this miracle of life and every single day I was with my marine brothers.

For their loved ones, my condolences. Have faith, even when it seems impossible at times because of the grief. They will be in Heaven guarding the pearly gates and smiling down on us.

Marines: To me, you were America's best. I will always feel honored to have served with you and walked among titans. RIP Warriors.

Manny Manoukian is Gone But Not Forgotten.

Manny and I served with the 1/6 "HARD" Infantry in Falluja. There are many others like Manny who made the ultimate sacrifice. Manny was extremely loyal and hardworking. He was one of the very best our country has to offer. RIP brother, you will be missed and never forgotten.

Brian Balduf is Gone But Not Forgotten.

Brain was a friend of mine who I served with in the 22d MEU (Marine Expeditionary Unit) who also died in combat from multiple tours. Brian was the epitome of a US Marine. Brain had a wife and kids and he will be missed.

RIP Brian.

Ronald Payne is Gone But Not Forgotten.

Ronald was the first casualty of war that I experienced while in Afghanistan. We served in the 22d MEU. I remember the utmost respect and reverence we had while loading him on the plane.

RIP Hard Charger. GBNF.

Doc Kent is Gone But Not Forgotten.

1/6 Infantry Navy Corpsmen. The one Sailor considered by all to be equal to a Marine in combat is a Navy Corpsmen.

RIP Doc Kent.

Hugo Espinoza is Gone But Not Forgotten.

There are veterans who die fighting their inner battles like Hugo Espinoza. I remember Hugo being meritorious promoted on the USS Wasp out on float in the Mediterranean coming back from Afghanistan. Hugo was an outstanding Marine. Hugo had a wife and kids and will be missed. I hope others who are fighting their inner battles get the help they need. RIP Hugo.

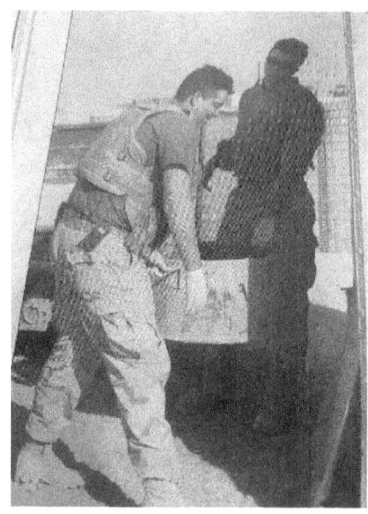

Joe Castillanos is Gone But Not Forgotten.

Joe always had a smile and his face. He was a very hard worker. He did his time honorably, then went back to Houston with his family and got a job in the post office. He was killed by Houston Police Department in front of his wife and two young girls while having a PTSD episode on Memorial Day.

RIP Joe you are GBNF.

21

Tools and Resources.

Tools and Resources.

Brewer's Association
https://www.brewersassociation.org/

Home Brewer's Association
https://www.homebrewersassociation.org/

Google Grow and the V badge
Google has fantastic tools of all kinds—and it's free! If you're a Veteran-owned or Veteran-led business, you can get the V badge on your business listing.
https://grow.google

Small Business Administration (SBA)
The U.S. Small Business Administration is also great! They have resources to help in everything from getting a business loan to education.
https://www.sba.gov/

LiftFund
LiftFund is truly a great organization that helps fund small businesses and has a plethora of resources for education.
https://www.liftfund.com/

22

Glossary.

Glossary.

atole – Cornmeal-based breakfast drink served warm.

calientito – Mexican Christmas fruit punch.

carnitas – Taco filling of slow-barbecued pork and slow-fried pork parts.

chamoy – Sauce that is typically spicy, pickled, sweet, sour, and salty—in other words, the best thing ever!

chicharrones – Fried pork cracklings.

clamato – Spicy tomato-based drink.

comal – Flat griddle primarily used for heating tortillas.

discada – Mixed meat dish served as tacos, cooked on a disc outside for grilling out.

machitos – Mexican street tacos made in different ways. The best I've had was made with chopped goat organs wrapped in goat intestine (trust me).

michelada – drink typically made with beer, lime, salt, and hot sauce.

migas – fried tostada chips, scrambled eggs, and salsa, usually made as tacos or scooped up to eat with tortillas

molotes – fried bread that is stuffed usually with meat

or cheese and shaped like a half circle from folding over the circular bread shape.

Reinheitsgebot — German purity law that limits the ingredients of beer to water, barley, yeast, and hops.

tepache – Fermented beverage made today typically with water, pineapple skins, and spices such as cinnamon and cloves.

tripitas – Mexican fried tripe. Sounds weird to some Americans, but it's *so good*!

23

List of Titles & Table of Recipes.

List of Titles.

How to Read this Book 5
Sundown on a Chapter in My Life 7
Part One: The Story Of Sun Brewing
Ingredients 12
Becoming El Guapo 15
Everything Under the Sun 22
Part Two: Cooking With El Guapo
There's No Such Thing as a Recipe 28
You, Too, Can Learn to Cook with Beer 35
Part Three: El Guapo's Brew Kettle
Beer Brewing Tips & Procedures 43
Sun Brewing Clone Recipes 56
My First Sun Beers 59
Classic Ales 66
Classic Lagers 89
Seasonals 97
Award-Winning Beers 106
Quintessential Borderland Avant-garde Ales 119

100% Spontaneous Ales 138
My Weird Beers 147
My Lunatic Series of Beers 160
Part Four: El Guapo's Kitchen
Borderland Avant-garde and Fusion Food 169
My Fermented Food 189
Preservation 202
My Borderland Backyard-Style Barbecue 216
Borderland Barbecue Recipes 222
Whole Animal Barbecue 235
Everything Else 244
Final Thoughts 294
Taking Brewing from Hobby to Community 295
Get to Know the Craft 296
History of Beer in El Paso 296
Get to Know the People Who Make the Laws 303
Giving Back 304
Giving Thanks 307
Letter to Fallen Marines 310
Tools and Resources 316
Glossary 317

Table of Recipes.

El Guapo's Brew Kettle

My First Sun Beers

    Meados de Alien Ale 59

Intercourse Ale 62
Sun IPA 63
Tamale Top Ale 64

Classic Ales

Left Turn at Albuquerque Pale Ale 66
Atreyu Belgian Pale Ale 68
Falkor Belgian Amber Ale 68
Nincompoop Continuously Hopped IPA 70
Gypsy Dude IPA 72
You Don't Know Jack! Fruit IPA 73
Canutillo Malt Liquor 75
Ard Draoi Irish Red 77
Holy Huerache Amber Ale 78
Old School Love Altbier 79
The Working Man Ice Ale 80
Wocka Wocka Brown Ale 83
Woo-woo Brown Porter 83
Cheeky Devil Tropical Stout 84
Angels' Share Foreign Extra Stout 86
Sun Arkhangelisk Russian Imperial Stout 87

Classic Lagers

Sun Black Ice Lager 90
The Third Edge Vienna Lager 92
Sun American Lager 94
O'Slocum's Red Malt Beverage 95

Seasonals

> **Valentine's Day**
> The People of the Sun Jamaica Ale 97
> **Halloween**
> Cinderella Loves Ale 98
> Canutillo Hoppy Vampires' Brew 100
> Frankenstein Hybrid Ale 101
> **Christmas**
> Sun Calientito Ale 103
> Gingerbread Man Ale 103
> Meados de Santa Claus 104

Award-Winning Beers

> Tepache Tamarindo Ale 106
> Saison de Membrillo 110
> Charlemagne's Holy Grail 100% Spontaneous Ale 112
> Beauregard Ice Dark Lager 117

Quintessential Borderland Avant-garde Ales

> Tepache Sour Ale 120
> Tepache IPA 121
> Tamarindo Ale 123
> Tamarindo Porter 124
> Chamoy Ale 125
> Huitlacoche Wildflower Ale 126

Green Mole Ale 127
Atole Breakfast Stout 128
Vagabundo Ale 129
Nicodemus Ale 130
Gypsies' Brew 132
Gypsies' Beer Music Gruit 133
Mesquite Bean Ale 134
Meados de Alien Lager 135
Green Chamoy Pickle Sour Lager 136

100% Spontaneous Ales.

Beyond the Pale 143
100% Spontaneous Tepache Ale 144
100% Spontaneous 6th Anniversary Tamale Top Ale 145
Illegitame non Carborundom Ale 146

My Weird Beers.

The Fozzie Lime Stout 147
Avocado Sour Ale 148
Vertigo Ale 150
Nirvana Russian Kvas 151
Green Chamoy Pickle Ale 151
Symposius Sour Porter 152
Narama Ancho Chile Sour Ale 153
Swords & Ale 155
Wasshoppening Wild Malt Liquor 156

Le Cygne Noir Black Saison 158
Wildling Ale 159

My Lunatic Series of Beers.

Lunatic Hopped Voodoo Cock Ale 160
Mole Madre Ale 162
Three Little Pigs Porter 163
Spicoli Ale 164

El Guapo's Kitchen

Pub Beer Food.

Tripitas Dog 170
Barbacoa Burger 171
Brisket Waffle Sandwich 175
Beer-Battered Frog Legs 176
Sun Brewing Tacos 179
Discada Tacos 181
Beer-nuts Battered Fried Pork Chops 183
3rd Anniversary Rum Raisin Tamales 185
6th Anniversary Chocolate Fig Tamales 188

My Fermented Food.

The Fermented Sope 189
Fermented Beer Batter-Fried Chicken 192
Fermented Chamoy Eggs 193

Sun Brewing's Hot Sauce 195
100% Spontaneous Fermented Bread 197
100% Spontaneous Fermented Bread made with Ale, Jalapeños, and Ganache 200

Preservation.

Frankenstein Grape Jelly 203
Mezcal Ancho Chile Guava Marmalade 205
Tepache Jalapeño Pickles 206
Chile Red Cabbage 209
Pickled Grilled Carrots 211
Chile Toreados 214

Borderland Barbecue Recipes.

Pipian Short Ribs 223
Chamoy Wings 223
Stout Beer-Battered Wings 225
Tamarindo Chicken 226
Tomahawk Steak 227
Texas Beer Brisket 229
Thanksgiving Beer-Injected Turkey and Granny's Stuffing 230
Granny's Thanksgiving Stuffing 231

Whole Animal Barbecue.

Horse Trough Whole Hog 235

Pulling some pork and Pig Head tacos 240
Goat Roast 241
Carving some goat and Tacos de Cabeza 243

Soups.

Stout Beer Goat Stew 244
Beer & Barley Oxtail Soup 246
Brewer's Barley Bread Bowl 247
Beer Nuts Cereal 259

Salads.

Chilendrina 251
Brewer's Salad 252

Dressings.

Tepache & Olive Oil Dressing 255
Blood Orange IPA Poppy Seed Dressing 256

Sides.

Brisket Elote Beer Crinkle Fries 257
Mexican Corn-in-a-Cup 259
Sour Beer & Salt Potato Chips 260
Ana's Drunken Charro Beans 262

Beer Breads.

> Sun Brewing's Stout Beer Tortillas 264
> Pale Ale Pretzels 265
> Saison Fougasse 267
> Brewer's Bread 269

Sauces.

> Sun Brewing's Beer Mustard 271
> Sun Brewing's Beer Mole 272
> Sun Brewing's Green Mole 274
> Sun Brewing's Tamarindo Salsa 275
> Porter Tamarindo Sauce 276
> Sun Brewing's Chamoy Sauce 277
> Sun Brewing's Green Chamoy Sauce 278
> Sun Brewing's Beer BBQ Sauce 279
> Sun Brewing's Hog Sauce 280
> Stout Beer Ganache 280
> Tepache Vinegar 281

Beverages.

> Tepache 282
> Russian Kvas 283
> Atole 283
> Calientito 284
> Pappy Slocum's Beer Nog 285

Desserts.

> Stout Chocoflan Cake 288
> Saison Ice Cream 290
> Beer Soufflé Ice Cream Sandwich 291

www.ingramcontent.com/pod-product-compliance
Lightning Source LLC
Chambersburg PA
CBHW051418290426
44109CB00016B/1345